Alyssa Tils

Thank you

Rocky Mountain Summit.

Please don't hesitate to reach out if you need some help with your digital marketing and public Relations.

Peter - 903-462-1160

TRUE CONNECTIONS

RELATIONSHIP MARKETING
IN THE DIGITAL WORLD

Martin Greif

Copyright © 2020 Martin Greif.

All rights reserved. No part of this book may be reproduced, stored, or transmitted by any means—whether auditory, graphic, mechanical, or electronic—without written permission of the author, except in the case of brief excerpts used in critical articles and reviews. Unauthorized reproduction of any part of this work is illegal and is punishable by law.

This book is a work of non-fiction. Unless otherwise noted, the author and the publisher make no explicit guarantees as to the accuracy of the information contained in this book and in some cases, names of people and places have been altered to protect their privacy.

ISBN: 978-1-71694-336-2 (sc)
ISBN: 978-1-71694-333-1 (e)

Library of Congress Control Number: 2020906930

Because of the dynamic nature of the Internet, any web addresses or links contained in this book may have changed since publication and may no longer be valid. The views expressed in this work are solely those of the author and do not necessarily reflect the views of the publisher, and the publisher hereby disclaims any responsibility for them.

Any people depicted in stock imagery provided by Getty Images are models, and such images are being used for illustrative purposes only. Certain stock imagery © Getty Images.

Lulu Publishing Services rev. date: 04/14/2020

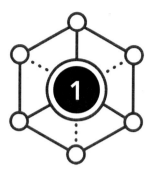

IT'S NOT ABOUT YOU!

We All Are a Selfish Lot!

It can be argued humans, just like animals, are inherently selfish. Though you can have a range of other emotions, this instinct to think about one's self has been displayed right from the prehistoric cavemen to the scientists of today. It is all about striving to make life better in some way, to make the chances of survival higher, therefore, ensuring one's lineage is preserved for future generations. This trait of selfishness is not exclusive to any species. All animals have the biological need to be selfish in order to win the survival race.

Imagine what it would have been like to be a caveman living in prehistoric times. If you found food, you would eat it yourself or share it only with your tribe. If threatened, cavemen would wield their clubs and deal with the threat in order to save themselves because survival was a priority. They had to put themselves first!

Times have changed. Today, you are a much more evolved species. The basic survival instinct is still there. However, it's in a dormant state because your survival is not threatened very often in the modern world. The constant fear of being eaten by a predator might not consume the thoughts of modern humans as it did for the club-wielding caveman. But you still need to survive, don't you? The world has changed a lot and the game of survival has changed too. Your selfish goal today is not just to stay alive but to have a better life. Your goal now is to be able to do better than others so you can have that sought-after job promotion, buy a dream house, or get a pay raise.

What about Selflessness?

The truth about selflessness is that it doesn't exist. All human actions stem from some self-interest. You often balk at the notion all people are selfish. Sometimes you do not seek material things, but that does not mean that self-interest isn't the goal. When you decide to forgive someone who has harmed you in some way, are you being the paragon of selflessness by doing it for that person? Or, are you forgiving that person so you can find peace within yourself? You need to let go of the burden on your soul, but you want to believe you are doing an act of kindness for someone else.

The word *selfish* might seem a little harsh in this context, but philosophers have long rationalized self-interest dictates everything you do, and the experts tend to agree. Each action can be viewed as a building block to help achieve your personal goals, both big and small. Even though the opinion is divided on whether this is a good thing or a bad thing, you cannot escape the fact that your basic instinct is to protect your self-interest.

Think about it for a moment. Some of you give to charities. Some of you are always there to help family or friends. Some of you go out of your way to lend a helping hand to a colleague. You are often good to other people! But, if you break down these little acts of kindness, what you are doing is trying to satisfy your need to do good and feel good. The fact that someone else is also benefiting from these acts is a bonus, but at a subconscious level, you do these things for yourself. This is the reason why people readily make donations to charities. This is the reason why major corporations engage in activities demonstrating corporate social responsibility. It is their way of giving back to the society from which they have taken resources to build their businesses. This is what brings them the satisfaction of doing something good for others while making the taking part easier.

Let's look at Maslow's Hierarchy of Needs to better understand how you always act with a selfish motive.

Maslow's Hierarchy of Needs

In 1943, American psychologist Abraham Maslow proposed the theory commonly known as Maslow's Hierarchy of Needs, also known as Maslow's pyramid. It not only explains human behavior, but also suggests how your actions are driven by your own various needs. This theory is probably one of the most widely accepted theories that supports the idea that humans act out of self-interest more than anything else.

Maslow's theory suggests once you have enough food to eat and a roof over your head, you want to be surrounded by loving people to give you a feeling of belonging. This is what pushes you to do good for others. You might not acknowledge it at times, but your instinct to be kind and helpful to others stems from your own need to receive kindness and be helped when you are in need. You expect reciprocation, in some form, for all your good deeds. Even if you are helping someone whom you know won't be able to extend the same help to you, you do it because of the belief that what goes around, comes around, and you always want good things to find their way back to you.

Once the basic social needs are fulfilled, then comes the need for recognition. You all want to be recognized for good work and appreciated for your efforts. You all want respect and a good social standing. It's no longer about staying alive; it's a much more complex need. This is the need that distinguishes you from animals. At this stage, people are confident their basic needs for survival are taken care of. You do not need to think about where the next meal is coming from, or whether you will have a roof over your head tomorrow. What you now need is more than mere survival. You need recognition in the eyes of other people; you need appreciation and praise.

At the top of Maslow's pyramid is the need to look good in one's own eyes—the need for self-actualization. At this point, one already has a solid social standing and earned the respect of others by exhibiting good behavior. Now, you want to prove to *yourself* that you are truly good. You want to do things that bring satisfaction and gratification, and your actions are driven by the need to please themselves.

If you look at the top half of the pyramid, it will explain the motivation behind even the smallest acts of kindness, which often seem selfless on the surface, are about fulfilling a person's own needs. This means when a person willingly donates money to a charity, you are doing it to demonstrate to the world you are generous. You want recognition and appreciation for it, or you do it for the satisfaction and happiness you personally get out of it. Similarly, when a teacher puts their soul into teaching a student, the teacher is probably looking for satisfaction that comes when the student does well. When a scientist forgets everything and immerses themself in research, they likely want the new discovery as proof of their own efforts, knowledge, and the recognition it would bring them.

The above are examples of the good that comes from the human trait of safeguarding one's self-interest. However, a lot of bad habits also stem from this trait.

The Bad Part of Selfishness

If you look within yourself, a lot of your bad habits are also a result of your selfishness. Let's look at some of these bad habits.

1. You love to talk about yourself and the things that interest you. Notice how some people can go on and on about themselves? About the places they have visited. About the books they have read. You all know that one person who cannot stop talking about how incredibly adorable their child is!

2. What happens when the people described above are at the receiving end of a conversation? They tend to interrupt, lose interest in the

conversation, and during the conversation, think how much the other person bores them.

3. You all like to be called by your name. Despite that, it is so often you forget the names of the people you just met, without acknowledging you, too, might share a similar attachment to their own names. You feel offended when someone forgets your name, misspells it, or pronounces it wrong, yet at the same time, when you do the same with someone else's name, you don't realize it's a problem.

4. You are extremely concerned about the things which give you happiness. For instance, an avid reader will not stop raving about the new book they have read but would be quick to lose interest when someone tells them about the new knitting technique, they learned online.

5. You worry about your own happiness all the time and strive to safeguard it. No matter how kind-hearted you are, the thoughts of your own happiness consume you much more than the thoughts of the happiness you can give others.

6. You all want that promotion along with the pay raise it comes with, but not everybody can have that. If you aren't chosen for the promotion, you are jealous of the co-worker who is.

7. You feel the need to have the best, so you often envy friends and neighbors who buy a better house, drive a better car, or get a better television.

These examples serve to demonstrate how selfishness can lead to bad behavior and are damaging to relationships—both personal and professional.

Nobody is perfect and everybody has bad habits. The problem arises when these bad habits get in the way of your day-to-day relationships and you are not able to bond with others because you are too absorbed in fulfilling your own goals. Humans are social animals, and it goes without saying relationships form an integral part of our lives.

But Why Talk about This Here?

From the child who finishes homework quickly in order to get a sweet treat to the old person who gives generously to the hospital's trust in their Will, are all acting on an instinct which forms the essence of human nature. Digital marketers, being human, also act with similar motives. After all, it's how you are all wired.

The important point to remember here, though, is Digital Marketing is a game you don't play alone, so how would it work to think only about yourself? Marketing professionals are trained in thinking from various perspectives. They know the rules of the game, but when the selfish nature comes into play in the marketing world, even the wisest marketers sometimes fail to build lasting relationships with their customers. There are times when their own goals blind them so much they are often unable to see beyond their own needs. They forget the customers also have their own self-interests to fulfill!

I wish I could say I am immune to this, but I'm only human, with the same biological programming as every other human being to instinctively think about what *I* want first! However, I'll say this much for myself: a few years ago, I read a couple of great books that changed my way of thinking. One was Dale Carnegie's *How to Win Friends and Influence People* and the other was *What Women Want Men to Know* by Barbara DeAngelis. These two books helped me understand human nature in detail. It made me aware of the many aspects of the complex human mind. These books helped me to understand that even though you would like things to be straightforward when it comes to human behavior, this is seldom how things work out. Above all, these books helped me to appreciate relationships are important and if you are willing to leave your selfish goals aside, it is quite easy to bond with people. This knowledge changed my entire worldview. It made me more conscious of other people's emotional needs and it helped me with my interactions not just in my personal life, but also formed the basis of my philosophy for business and marketing.

TRUE CONNECTIONS

When you are consumed by your own objectives or desires, you might be able to focus on little else. You must push pass to look at the bigger picture.

Years ago, I worked for a division of a large corporation as Director of Marketing. In this position I had a few opportunities to test my philosophy in real life. Although they have evolved over time the basis of this book started here.

The division I worked in created and sold high-performance databases to run on the DEC Vax platform. Prior to joining, they created a lead generation campaign that was perfect in every way except for the offer. The campaign described the business problems faced by organizations needing a high-performance database and then, in exchange for their contact information, they offered a Thesaurus and Dictionary set. This generated a return of almost 7%, which was unheard of back then. When I asked how many of these leads became sales, or even prospects, I was greeted with blank stares. Not a single real sales cycle was created, which meant this campaign was a failure. Yet, the original marketing piece was terrific. Armed with the knowledge that this offer had failed; I created a new offer: an excerpt chapter from a well-respected book about high-performance databases. Of course, the return rate dropped to less than 2%, but these were mostly qualified prospects. If you are marketing high-performance databases, anyone who wants a chapter on high-performance databases falls into one of three categories:

1. They have no life.

2. They are a prospect.

3. They have no life and are a prospect.

I joke here, but the reality is someone interested enough to ask for dry technical information on database management systems is probably worth talking to when marketing a high-performance database. By focusing on the needs of the recipients and crafting the offer to attract those whose needs we could meet, this marketing campaign became a win/win.

Years later, the company decided to fold multiple software divisions into one company. The division was going to be downsized by over 60%, which meant a lot of people would lose their jobs. I devised a plan to buy the division and asked my team to help. To make this work, we had to continue to market the software so the division would be successful after the buyout. My team continued to come in early and work late knowing they might well lose their jobs. My team trusted me.

Unfortunately, I could not make the plan a reality and most of my team lost their jobs. I then spent the next two months helping each one of them find new positions at other companies. Even though I also lost my job, I had to help these people. Did I do it because I was selfless? No. I did this because at my core, I needed to. I was responsible for asking them to work hard even though they were most likely going to lose their jobs. I could not focus on looking for a new position for myself until after I had helped them. This is the top of Maslow's hierarchy. As I was financially stable, I did not drop down lower in the pyramid. I was helping others in order to help me feel good about myself. At the time I did not realize this, and in fairness, many of you don't know why you do what you do. In retrospect however, this was exactly what I was doing.

Both examples were right before Internet Marketing blossomed, but the theories behind old-school marketing are valid today.

Self-Interest and Relationship with Others

If humans are inherently self-interested, then why do you crave connections with others?

You may recall the need to belong ranks third up in Maslow's Hierarchy of Needs. If people need to feel acceptance from others, then their actions towards the fulfillment of this need are not necessarily in conflict with their self-interest. Someone who seeks peer approval, for instance, will do everything to ingratiate themselves with their peers. They may engage in big-hearted gestures or be more generous with praise to others. They will do everything to mirror the values of the group they are trying to be a part of. And they may do all these unconsciously.

So, the actions people do to feel connected to others - including acts of kindness and generosity - ultimately benefits themselves in the end. Psychologists note that social connection enhances self-esteem and bolsters feelings of being valued. In turn, this sense of being valuable to others contributes to increased feelings of happiness.

Psychological Egoism

The central role of self-interest as a driving force behind human desire and motivation is at the core of Psychological Egoism, which is a paradigm that has fascinated great thinkers for centuries. Psychological Egoism dates to ancient Greek civilization, when Socrates discussed human self-centeredness with his brother Glaucon. Glaucon famously argued that people engaged in good behavior (i.e. not harming others) mainly for self-preservation and out of fear of punishment. When the threat of punishment is absent, people are bound to act according to their own selfish nature, regardless of the consequences to others.

This argument was echoed several centuries later by other philosophers, notably British Reformation political thinker, Thomas Hobbes. In *Leviathan*, Hobbes declares even voluntary acts like helping others or doing one's duty have ulterior motives, the simplest of which is the person's own pleasure derived from such acts.

More contemporary thinkers echo this notion include the famous psychoanalyst Sigmund Freud. Freud believed human nature was fundamentally animalistic and ego-centric, concerned mainly with pleasure-seeking and pain avoidance. According to him, social norms, rules and regulations were necessary to control the impulses of humans, without which society would descend into chaos and anarchy as everyone sought to pursue only their self-interest.

A similar perspective can be found in Ayn Rand's novel *Atlas Shrugged*, where the protagonist reflects the author's argument humans are fundamentally selfish by nature and individuals exist only for the sake of themselves. Rand's position is like Maslow's, where the achievement of personal happiness (self-actualization) is the highest moral purpose for human existence.

Undoubtedly, these perspectives from the psychological egoist camp have often been controversial. After all, selfishness is usually cast as a negative quality in a person. Therefore, Psychological Egoism is often attacked for reducing humans to their insensitive sides. However, denying this aspect of human nature is tantamount to denying an important facet of what it means to be human and accepting its puzzling complexity. You might not behave out of self-serving interests all the time, but that does not mean you don't do so most of the time, especially when you are operating on autopilot (a.k.a. NOT thinking).

Selfishness and Building Relationships

As a marketer, it pays to learn these lessons from psychology when you are trying to build a relationship with your prospects and existing customers.

You must acknowledge the fact that your actions will inevitably be influenced by your selfishness. This way, you can watch yourself when you're making significant decisions that affect other people. Be conscious about the possible negative effects of being perceived as too self-serving by your employees and customers. No one likes to be in a one-way relationship, not in romantic ones and certainly not in business.

Bear in mind that those around you have their own selfish motivations. So, when you're trying to build a relationship with business partners and customers, be ready to meet certain expectations on how the relationship will be mutually beneficial for everyone involved. Put the principle of reciprocity to action: satisfy the selfish needs of others in any relationship and they will be more willing to reciprocate and return the favor of being a valuable partner or customer.

TRUE CONNECTIONS

From the Perspective of Digital Marketing

Traditional marketing relies on relationships to a great extent. For instance, take your neighborhood store. Let's look at an ideal scenario in traditional marketing:

You enter the store. Someone greets you pleasantly and asks you what you are looking for. Based on your answer, you are led to the appropriate area in the store where a friendly salesperson strikes a conversation with you. They help you with choosing the right product and find it for you. They also make you aware of any discounts or offers the store is running. You sense the salesperson has good knowledge about the product, and when you ask them questions about the product, they can answer them. They help you in selecting the right product for your needs.

Once you select the product, they ask you whether they could help you with anything else and they even suggest other products based on your current purchase, or, if you're a regular customer, your previous purchases. Then, when you have selected the items you wish to purchase, they help you with the payment process, ensuring it is quick and seamless.

Just like that, you are on your way, satisfied with the purchase and with the help you received during the process! You would probably want to return to this store for future purchases. You are also quite likely to recommend the store to your friends and family. It goes without saying that this good experience for the customer works wonders for the store in question.

A physical store is quite different from a website that only sells online. From a customer's point of view, there are definite advantages of buying from a brick and mortar store:

1. The trust factor is easy — you get what you see.

2. You can't replace the experience of *see and touch* an actual store provides.

3. In many cases, you can take the product home with you right away – no waiting for the delivery.

4. The interaction between the customer and the seller is *real* therefore, more comforting.

However, even though the digital world has some definite shortcomings, it is anything but a lost cause. There are many reasons why people choose or do not choose to buy online, but one cannot deny the effect an actual interaction can have on the customer. As a seller meeting a customer in person, there is so much you can do to establish a bond with the customer. What do you get in return? You get the customer's loyalty for life, assuming you are successful in establishing that bond. You get more customers for your business and courtesy recommendations from satisfied customers.

So, you would think Digital Marketing pales in comparison, right? You couldn't be more wrong here! Why do you suppose Digital Marketing has to be cold and impersonal? Just because there is no physical interaction with the customer, does not mean you cannot form a relationship with them. It does not mean it is impossible to establish trust and it does not mean you cannot make customer loyalty and retention a reality!

Digital Marketing is in no way less effective than traditional marketing. There are definite advantages of an online business from the point of view of a business owner:

1. No need to invest in rent or purchase of an actual store.

2. No investment for buying infrastructure.

3. No maintenance charges.

4. It is possible to customize service for a lot of customers at the same time without having as many salespeople.

5. The analytics tools make it easy to track sales or conversions and get reports, which can be very helpful in making changes to the marketing strategy.

We have already established people are very self-centered. When, as a marketer, you are looking at generating leads or converting leads into customers, you are looking at dealing with people. It really helps to know the common traits of people. It helps to know what drives them and it helps to know what the motivation behind their actions are because ultimately, you want them to *take the conversion action*. So, you need to know how to motivate them to take this action.

You really need to understand the thought process behind every action. You need to keep in mind how every action is a result of wanting to fulfill one's needs.

But first, let's see how you are instinctively inclined to run a bad marketing campaign.

How Bad Habits Can Affect Digital Marketing

Business owners often have some preconceived ideas when they design their websites. They know what they want, and they have already visualized what the website should look like. They have certain expectations from the website, which they want to see in the results.

This is exactly where they go wrong!

Customers are the ones who are going to judge the website. It might be perfect from the marketer's point of view, but if it does not work well for the customers, it is not of any use. It is natural, due to the inherent human nature, to always put your own interests first. When you cannot shake off your tendency for selfishness, it gives rise to some very bad habits in marketing.

MARTIN GREIF

Let me share an experience I had a few years ago:

I was looking for some material for my research. As I typed the relevant string in the search engine and hit enter, I was met with the usual array of websites. While browsing through the list, one of the websites caught my attention. It claimed to have the best material in the industry on the subject, in the form of a downloadable white paper. I opened the website in anticipation, hoping I had finally reached the right place. There was some information about what I might expect in the downloadable material – an excerpt of sorts. I started reading the excerpt trying to figure out what was there when about two seconds later a large pop-up appeared, obscuring the text I was in the middle of reading. This very ill-mannered pop-up then informed me I needed to sign-up before I could access the material. I decided to take a gamble because I really needed some good material for my research. *"Let's get this over with"*, I said to myself and clicked on the large *Sign Up* button. Imagine my disappointment when I was met with one of the most exhaustive forms that asked for just too many details, including seemingly unimportant bits such as where I work, my age, and my interests relevant to the subject I was researching. Looking at the information I was expected to share with a random website, my disappointment soon turned to annoyance. What does the download have to do with my phone number, for instance?

Undoubtedly, the people behind this preposterous form were acting simply out of their own self-interest. Their website design and the clever idea to generate leads before allowing for a download clearly gave away, they were thinking only about themselves. From a customer's point of view, that is a huge turn off. A marketer that comes across as selfish will seldom be able to attract customers. Even if by some miracle they can generate leads or get customers, it is highly unlikely the customers will come back to them, assuming the product they are marketing is available elsewhere.

In case you are still wondering, no, I did not go through with the tedious registration process. I simply kept looking until I found a website delivering what they promised. They let me download the material from their website, no questions asked.

Like the example above, there are many things marketers do that scream selfish! Let's look at some annoying habits you often see on websites:

1. Compulsory registration before a visitor can access website content.

2. Giving the visitors unnecessary details about special discounts and offers, which might not be relevant to them.

3. While the customer is in the process of purchasing, jumping on them with cues to "like" their page on social media, or nudging a buyer-in-progress to share the page with their friends.

4. Asking for too much information during the lead generation process, often including questions that do not seem relevant to what the visitor is looking for.

5. Confusing the visitors with too much content, which they find neither interesting nor helpful.

6. Bragging too much about how they provide the best products or services on the market.

7. Trying to fit everything on the webpage so visitors don't miss a thing. The result is a cacophony of colors and things flashing at you or popping up without warning.

Why Are Digital Marketers Selfish?

Do Digital Marketers want to be selfish? Are Digital Marketers truly bad people who make selfish decisions, then sit in their offices and laugh about it? Hardly. All they want is to make the marketing campaign work! They do everything they can possibly think of to make a great campaign, but the fact remains not all marketing campaigns are successful.

Let's look at some of the reasons behind selfish marketing strategies:

1. The Digital Marketer often works on the suggestions and requirements of the business owner. However, the business owner is not a marketing expert and their expectation of how the website must look might be largely based on their self-interest.

2. When a lot of time and effort is spent on developing content for the website, it becomes difficult to let a large part of it go. In order to keep most of the content on the website, the marketers often end up crowding too much content on the webpage.

3. When a gifted marketer devises a clever marketing strategy of cross-selling, they can't help but want to try the same strategy with every potential customer, which often disregards the customer's needs.

4. The marketer has come up with several discount offers to lure customers. The marketer then thinks it is necessary to bombard every visitor to the site with the details of various offers because the offers are so good!

5. A good Digital Marketer is aware of the power of social media for improving the brand value as well as reaching a wider audience. This is how they justify taking every opportunity to hound visitors to Like/Share/Comment/Follow on their social media pages.

What Digital Marketers Need to Understand?

We have spoken extensively about how people are driven by selfish motives. But why should you care about this? Why should you keep selfishness in mind? Because of this simple reason: you, too, are driven by your selfish motives. The first step before you embark on your Digital Marketing journey is to understand that as far as your website is concerned, *it's not about you!*

TRUE CONNECTIONS

You might be tempted to think only about yourself and go ahead with your marketing campaigns. You might think avoiding mistakes like those mentioned earlier should be enough to bring in a decent number of clients for your business. Maybe you *could* achieve that but be assured the results would be short term, to say the least. Also, if the visitors do take the desired conversion action due to lack of alternatives, they are sure to jump ship when a rival business launches their website.

If you are looking only at short-term benefits, you are harnessing only a part of your website's potential. Empowered with the right attitude though, you can greatly increase conversions on your website. Let's repeat it again because it's so important to understand: the right attitude is to acknowledge *it's not about you!*

If you want to win customers for life – and that is always great for any business – it is imperative, you understand the psyche of your target audience.

It takes a lot of maturity to admit it's not about you. First, you need to admit it to yourself and then seamlessly incorporate this thought in your website design and your marketing strategy. Even if it's your business, it's not about you! When you reach the level of maturity where you don't make everything about yourself, you begin to look at the larger picture. You will then be able to keep your selfishness in check and think from a different perspective – a perspective which would make all the difference between good marketing and great marketing.

In the following chapters you will see exactly how you can overcome your selfishness for starting and maintaining a great Digital Marketing campaign. For now, suffice it to say if you are looking at developing real relationships with your customers, you should know how to focus on things other than those that interest *you!*

What Will You See in This Book?

In this book, you will learn how to form a connection with your customers, find out why this is important, and will understand what this can do for your business.

Below are the details of the rest of the chapters in this book you will come across:

Chapter 2 – Aligning user intent

If the marketer is selfish, the customer is selfish too. But who is right? In this chapter, you will see how both can be right, and how to turn this into a win/win situation.

Chapter 3 – The three things visitors ask themselves when they see your website

What are the questions a visitor would ask themselves when they land on your website? In this chapter, you will see what you can do to ensure they have favorable answers to the questions in their minds.

Chapter 4 – Marketing to the top of the funnel vs the bottom of the funnel

When you build your sales funnel, you want to have all bases covered. In this chapter, you will see how to accomplish this.

Chapter 5 – Persuasion

Persuading the customers to take the desired conversion action forms the crux of the marketing strategy. In this chapter, you will learn and understand the subtle art of persuasion.

Chapter 6 – Developing websites with mobile usage in mind

Currently, many people have moved primarily to smartphones for browsing and even making actual purchases. In this chapter, you will see why it is important to cater to the increasing number of mobile users and how exactly to go about it.

Chapter 7 – Using technology

The number of analytic tools and other technology available to Digital Marketers is one of the greatest advantages of Digital Marketing over traditional marketing. In this chapter, you will learn how to best use technology for the ultimate marketing campaign.

Chapter 8 – Stupid human tricks

What are the silly tricks Digital Marketers employ in their bid to increase sales? In this chapter, you will see why these tricks fail and what you should do instead.

Chapter 9 – All touchpoints

There is more to Digital Marketing than just designing good websites. In this chapter, you will explore the other elements of Digital Marketing such as E-mail Marketing, Social Media Marketing, etc. You will learn to ensure they all work together for your digital business.

Chapter 10 – Creating fans

At the end of the day, who doesn't want a happy ending? In this chapter, you will see how all your efforts towards building a relationship with the customers wins you fans for life.

ALIGNING USER INTENT

If self-interest forms the core of all *your* actions, then surely your audience is also motivated by the need to fulfill *their* self-interest? As a Digital Marketer you need to be able to see past your self-interest and think more about your audience.

For instance, if a visitor comes to a website looking for running shoes, they don't want to see moving banners announcing all styles of training shoes. The brand may have the best training shoes on the market, and they may have lots of happy purchasers, which the business must be proud of, but this visitor does not care about training shoes. They want running shoes. Period.

The important thing to remember is your visitors do not care about you and your wants. They care about themselves. Their concern about your website is limited to whether you can provide them with what they are looking for and if you can provide it within their budget. Maybe you are good at something, but if it is beyond the scope of their needs, it usually is of no interest to them. Why? Because, *they don't really care about you!*

But you, as a Digital Marketer, must care about them!

Using Traffic to Your Advantage

So, who do you think decides whether your website is great? Who are the experts? Someone from higher management in your organization? *No way!* The Digital Marketing expert? *Not really!* As simple as it may sound, it's your audience. They are the ones who are really judging your website. They will judge the services you offer, the products you sell, your emails, your social media ads…everything! And since they are judging you, remember it's *their* verdict that matters. As you can see, it's not about you – it's about *them*.

Being successful in driving traffic to your website is great but, know how to use this traffic to your advantage. A smart marketer knows how to tune in to what the audience has to say, and if you know where to look, this traffic is going to help you understand what improvements your website needs. Good traffic means you have enough data to be able to understand the audience.

One of the major advantages of Digital Marketing is the ability to track your traffic. With the right analytics tools, you can easily find the source of your traffic, the demographic of your website's visitors, the bounce rate, the conversion rate, and other metrics. You can use this data to support your decisions and strategies. So, use the traffic data on your website wisely.

Who is Your Audience? – Know Your Customer

The very first step of marketing is knowing who the audience is that would be interested in what you are promoting.

Let's suppose, for example, you have a website selling activity boxes for young children. Who is your audience? Your primary target audience are probably young parents, in their thirties or early forties. They would be the ones most interested in your product. Sure, you could have grandparents wanting to purchase the activity boxes for their grandchildren, or you could have other friends and relatives wanting to gift the boxes to young children. But, when you design the website and plan the marketing strategy, you need to keep in mind who the primary target audience is.

This is true for traditional marketing and the world of Digital Marketing is no different.

Let's start with the very basic things you need to know about the people you want to target when marketing your product or service. It could be as simple as knowing the age, gender, and race of the target group, or, you could really go into specifics. For instance, if you're selling brand new pickup trucks, according to recent market data, you would target men age 25 and older who own a house as these are the largest group of new truck buyers.

The more you know about your prospects, the better your targeting will be. And if you already have customers, you have a wealth of data which helps you in the following ways:

1. You already know your existing customers' preferences, but with this information, you would know your prospects better. Having this information allows you to focus your marketing strategies according to their specific needs.

2. You now have a way to see if the target group you initially identified for your product is in line with the actual customers you are drawing in. If not, you can fine-tune your target group and align your marketing strategy accordingly.

   For instance, you have a cooking website where you publish recipes. You probably worked out that your target audience would be women, between the ages of 18 and 50. But, through a survey on your website, you discover you're getting a lot of male visitors, too. You also discover the male visitors are more interested in the *Salads* section of your website. If you incorporate this knowledge in your marketing efforts, you can reach out to a wider audience and potentially increase your traffic.

3. When you advertise a product on social media and want to use images of people, it makes more sense to use images of people with whom your target group can identify. For instance, if you have a fitness program for which the target audience is senior citizens, you don't want to use pictures of young men with rippling muscles and young women in skimpy outfits showing off their abs and glutes.

It would be more appropriate if you would use images of men and women in their sixties, dressed in work-out clothes and looking fit.

From a selling point of view:

You need to know your customer well. If you don't know who your customer is, you are basically just putting your product out there to just wait and see who shows up to buy it. This is a very poor way to run a business. The customer is the backbone of your business. The only way your business can survive is if you have plenty of customers keeping it alive. So, when you say the customer is all important, it's a no brainer you need to know your customer really, *really*, well!

From a marketing point of view:

People today are relying more and more on the internet to look for things they need. But it makes no sense to market your product or service to every single person who uses the internet. You need to identify the select few who would be interested in you. Once you do that, then your time, energy, and resources will be focused in the right direction. That would make such a huge difference to your marketing strategy! Things would be so much simpler and straightforward.

Let's summarize all the benefits of knowing your audience well:

a) When you know what kind of people you are dealing with, and know enough about them, you can separate them into different categories. When this is done, you can move on to carefully segment your marketing strategies for each group with your newsletter emails, landing pages, or follow-up surveys.

b) You may have already identified your target group but, knowing your customers well will tell you whether your assumptions about the group are true.

c) If you fully understand your target group, you will know what you can do or say to win their trust and to get them interested in your business.

d) Knowing customers well and really bonding with them will help give your business valuable, lifetime customers. These are the people who keep coming back to you for all their needs within the boundaries of your business.

e) Happy, satisfied customers are more likely to promote your business within their own groups. By doing this, they are helping you to acquire leads, which potentially brings more customers.

How Do You Get to Know Your Customer?

There are two ways of knowing who will be interested in your business: instinct and data.

It's not bad to go with your gut feeling and map out your marketing strategy based largely on your instinct. Sometimes you just know how something you have to offer will click with the people out there. You know they will be interested in it, and you know they will either want to know more (leads) or go right for the purchase (customers). Basing your marketing strategy on instinct is fine, *if it works for your business.*

There is, however, a surefire way to know your customers: have the right tools to gather the statistics for you. But, it's always better not to rely on a single source to get to know your customers. Use multiple channels and integrate the data received from each to really understand the people you are currently doing business with or those you will potentially do business with.

a) Use web searches and do extensive, detailed market research.

b) You can even look to the online communities such as Quora or Reddit to understand the people you would profile in your target group.

c) Look at the people who are buying from your competitors.

d) Look at the customer reviews online for similar products. It gives you huge insights into exactly what the customer is looking for.

e) Surveys are a great way to understand people's expectations. You can either have your existing customers fill out survey forms, or you can have short surveys on your landing pages. This will allow potential leads to tell you what they need. You can even use other survey data available online.

Is Marketing Only About the Audience?

So, if it's not just about you, it is only about the customer, right? Well, yes, except for the *only* part. Marketing is about your customers, but not *just* about them. Marketing does not need to be a selfless act where you just work towards meeting the needs of your customers. Far from it! Look at it this way: when visitors go to a website, they are looking for something. If your website gives them an experience that can be aligned with what they want, i.e., they feel you will be able to provide what they are looking for, you have won half the battle. When you align *your* goals with what the customer needs, well, that is the perfect mix!

Successful marketing is all about understanding what the customer wants and making it available to them. It is also about being aware of the business goals. By looking out for everyone's needs, the interests of both the business owner and customer are protected.

A definite win/win wouldn't you say? Of course, that's easier said than done! But don't worry. In the following section, you will see how you can strike the perfect balance between your wants and your customers' needs.

The Three Steps for the Perfect Alignment

Step 1 – Identify your goals

When you set out to create the perfect website, what do you expect to get out of it? The goal could be to get leads, achieve sales, get subscriptions, or just create brand awareness. In any case, you need good traffic to your website. So, you invest in social media advertising or go for PPC (Pay Per Click) searches in order to attract visitors. You think everything is going fine, but then, you notice even though you are getting a good number of visitors, they are not taking the desired conversion action. *Why is there a gap?*

To bridge this gap, you not only need to understand the audience, but you also need to understand your goals. Unless and until you know what you want to achieve, how are you supposed to make it happen?

Knowing your goals is obviously the first step in mapping out your plan to achieve them. So, before you invest your time and money into a Digital Marketing campaign, you must first ask yourself *exactly* what you want to get out of it. While asking yourself this, be as specific as possible.

Do you have a specific sales target?

Are you looking at building your email list to a certain number of subscribers?

Is your goal to generate a certain amount of leads?

Do you want to create brand awareness among the audience?

Do you want to boost traffic to your website?

Whatever they are, be sure you write the goals down. It is very important not to lose your focus when working on your Digital Marketing strategies. Currently, the possibilities in Digital Marketing have increased so much it is easy to get lost in the maze. There are just so many strategies, and so many tools available it is better to focus on your goals. In this way, you can save time and money by employing only those methods which are best suited to achieve those goals.

But for that, you also need to know the economic value of your goals.

Assigning an Economic Value to Your Goals

At the end of the day, it's all about the monetary profits your business generates. That is why it is very important to assign an economic value to your goals.

For instance, if your goal is to generate a certain number of leads per week, you need to know the value each lead brings to your business. Anyone who shows interest in your business would be called a lead.

Before setting a goal of a certain number of leads in a certain timeframe, look at the leads you are getting now. At the risk of stating the obvious, you want the leads to take a conversion action. Knowing the number of leads and the number of conversions, you can find the conversion rate.

Let's explain this through an example: Suppose you have a website selling office furniture. You spend money on advertising your website, so what you essentially want to know, by calculating the value per lead, is whether the money being spent on advertising is giving you a good ROI (return on investment).

Conversion Rate = Total number of conversion actions / Total number of leads * 100 (Over a timeframe)

For example, let's say you have 200 visitors to your website during a one-week period, out of which 20 take the desired conversion action, which is to complete the purchase of furniture.

So now, your conversion rate can be calculated as follows:

Conversion Rate: (20/200) * 100 = 10

So, your conversion rate is 10%.

Now, look at the value of your total sales. This will help you calculate the value per lead.

Value per lead: sales value/number of leads

Suppose the total value of all unique purchases is $1000, then your value per lead would be calculated as below:

Value per lead: 1000/200 = 5

The value per lead is $5. In other words, in order to generate $1000, you would need an average of 200 leads.

But what is the relationship between lead value and conversion rate? Lead value is your average sale multiplied by your conversion rate:

Value per lead = Average sale value x Conversion rate

In the example above, if you made an average sale value of $50, and your conversion rate is 10%, then your value per lead would be: 50 x 10% = 5.

TRUE CONNECTIONS

Another important number you should know is the ROI (Return on Investment). Knowing the projected ROI helps give you a perspective on things. It helps you to adjust the amount of money you would be spending on website development, advertising, lead generation efforts, content generation, and other marketing activities.

Typically, the ROI is calculated using the below equation:

ROI = ((Conversion Value – Advertising Costs) / Advertising Costs) * 100

Taking from the example above, where the lead conversion value is $5, if you are spending $2.50 on advertising per lead, your ROI would be as below:

ROI = ((5-2.5)/2.5) * 100 = 100%

The above calculation is very basic but, when you sit down to put a value to your leads, you need more detailed statistics to assign an accurate value. This is because some leads would be more inclined to carry out the conversion action than others, which makes them more valuable to you. For this, you need to understand your leads well.

Understanding Lead Value

Not all leads are equal in importance because one lead could be more valuable than another. You need to take into consideration what types of leads you are getting in order to truly understand the value of these leads. Let's look at the different types of leads:

1. **Yes**
   These are the people who are very interested in what you have to offer. They hardly need any convincing. They are your satisfied customers who keep coming back. They are the people who have already been influenced by your marketing and trust in you. There is hardly any further effort required from your end at this point except for leading them through the purchase.

2. **Slightly Yes**
   These are the people who know about your business and trust you enough to consider buying from you. They aren't yet completely convinced but show definite potential. They need a little bit of nudging.

3. **Maybe**
   These are the ones who could have concerns like the "Slightly Yes", but you need to put it in some effort to convince them.

4. **Slightly No**
   These are the window-shoppers. They are interested in you, even if they do not have a clear intention of buying. They want to look around, but they are not going to be spending their money on you currently.

5. **No**
   These are the ones who were led to your website through clickbait, or maybe even they are unsure how they ended up at your website! These could also be your competitors who are looking at your price lists. Whatever the case, they are the ones that are not going to buy from you.

The above types of leads can also be classified according to the temperature of the leads. Something like the illustration below:

Hot	Warm	Cold

Definitely Yes   Slightly Yes   Maybe   Slightly No   **Definitely No**

1. From the above image, it is clear marketing to the Hot Leads would lead to better conversion rates, while marketing to the Cold Leads might not give you good conversions.

2. Also, the Hot Leads are the ones who are already convinced, so there is less of a marketing effort. They don't need too much

TRUE CONNECTIONS

convincing. The Cold Leads, on the other hand, might need a *lot* of convincing. But even then, they still might not convert.

3. The grey area (or should we say orange?) are the Warm leads you would need to work at in order to get the conversions. This area of your leads is also the widest so, if your marketing strategy is spot on, you are looking at a lot of conversions from this area.

Aside from the type of leads, the source of the leads also matters. Let's understand this through some examples.

We have already seen that:

Lead value = Average Sales Value / Total number of Leads

So, for example, if the total revenue for your company for the previous year was $5,373,550 and the total number of leads during that year is 3,416,384, this means the Lead Value is 5373550/3416384 = $1.57

But remember, not all leads have the same value. If you separate the leads based on the source from which those leads come from, you might have something like the table below:

Source	Leads	Sales	Lead Value
Social Media	1,314,283	$2,683,590	$2.04
Influencers	1,412,210	$2,254,642	$1.59
PPC	689,891	$435,318	$0.63
Total	**3,416,384**	**$5,373,550**	**$1.57**

See how knowing the source of your leads helps you get a better idea of which source is working better for you?

Just like the source of the leads, knowing the age of the leads is also important. Are newer leads performing better when compared to leads that have been on your lists for weeks, or even years? Or does your website depend heavily on repeat customers and the older leads, who tend to spend much more money as compared to the newer leads, who are more cautious?

If you look at the age of the leads and then find out how valuable they are, you might have something like this:

Age of the leads	Number of leads	Sales	Value of lead
Less than one year	708,234	$2,959,689	$4.17
1-2 years	901,245	$1,982,165	$2.20
More than 2 years	1,806,905	$431,696	$0.24
Total	3416384	$5373550	$1.57

Even though fictitious, the above table gives an idea of how things could look if, in certain businesses, newer leads prove to be more valuable.

Knowing the correct lead value helps you align your marketing efforts correctly. For example, if you know which type of leads work best for your business, and which leads have a poor value, you can concentrate your efforts on leads that have better chances of improving your conversions. Impact of improved conversion rates, through lead value could be dramatic. For instance, if you consider marketing as the only cost, and marketing cost per lead is $1, then a change in the value per lead can drastically improve your profits:

If value/lead = $1.25, Profit = $0.25

If value/lead = $1.5, Profit = $0.5

There is a 100% increase in the profit, just by improving the value/lead.

Having the correct lead value will help you arrive at the correct calculation of the number of leads you would need per sales cycle to achieve your target sales and/or revenue goals for a certain period.

Step 2 – Find out what your website visitors are looking for

Once you are perfectly clear about what you want and what the economic value of your goals are, you need to ask yourself the next important question: What are your website visitors looking for?

Continuing with the office furniture website from above, your primary goal is probably to offer state-of-the-art, modern furniture. Your website's objective is to reassure the customer they are at the right place to buy the furniture they are looking for and will get the best deal in terms of quality and affordability.

But are the visitors only coming with the intention to buy?

Or, are they on your site to compare prices?

Or, are they visiting to look at the designs you offer?

Or, do they just want to see what's new in the office furniture market?

Visitor intent can vary from case to case.

- **Buying**
  A user comes with the intent to buy a product or a service. They are not concerned with how the product is made, where it is stocked, etc.

- **Consuming Content**
  A visitor comes looking for content, such as research material, a white paper, an e-newspaper, a blog, etc.

- **Looking for Information**
  A visitor wants information. It could be help on how to get a task done, or pricing information, or comparison between the features of two products. It could also be information on where they can go to buy a product or a service. For example, the person may be looking

for the location of a physical store in order to buy something, a restaurant in which to eat, or a place to get their hair done.

- **Interaction**
  A visitor might simply want to interact with other people by signing up on a social media website, or by becoming a part of online communities, or posting opinions on review sites, etc.

Only when the visitor's intent is aligned with the content of the website will they find what they are looking for. An incorrect alignment, or a complete lack of it, means the visitor will be disappointed and leave quickly (bounce).

A lot of websites make the mistake of focusing only on traffic, but that is a very poor way of running a website. If the intent is not aligned, the bounce rate will significantly go up. The bounce rate also impacts the search engine rankings.

How Does One Determine User Intent?

User intent can be determined using any, or all, of the following:

- Analytics
- Surveys
- Exit Popups
- Heatmaps
- Session Recordings
- User Panels
- Interviews
- Chat
- Phone Calls
- Common Sense
- Touch Point Audits
- Content for Conversion Audits
- User Scenarios
- Testing

We will cover these methods in detail in Chapter 7.

Step 3 – Ensuring a good website experience for the visitors

A good website experience is the backbone of CRO. Aligning user intent on the website is definitely an important factor in ensuring a good website experience. However, there's more to it.

A good website experience is also about instilling trust in the visitor's mind and it is about helping the customer get what they want.

The Greedy Marketer Syndrome

Are you the greedy marketer? Read the following for a reality check:

- **You always focus only on the profits**
  If you have a business, it is a given that you must focus on how much money the website helps you make. And that is perfectly alright. The problem arises when all you think about is the profits. You are so blinded by the figures at the bottom of the balance sheet, you do not see anything else.

- **You don't want to take any risks**
  You have devised a marketing strategy that works well for your business and gives you consistent profits. You are happy with this model of business and don't want to take any risks involved when you make changes to your current strategy.

- **You don't think it's necessary to understand your audience**
  You don't feel the need to have a deeper understanding of your audience. You are content with the knowledge there is a set audience contributing to conversions on your website. You think it is a waste of resources to discover more about the audience, especially since you are satisfied with the conversions.

- **You don't believe in segmenting your strategy according to the type of audience**
  You are not ready to experiment with your marketing strategy. You are happy with the one-size-fits-all approach. You treat all

your visitors equally and are convinced this is working to your advantage.

- **You want to focus only on the hot leads**
  You know the hot leads bring in the most conversions, therefore, the most profits. So, you give in to the temptation of catering only to the needs of your hot leads. The returns are good, so you want to stick with this strategy.

- **You want your website to sustain only on the primary conversion actions**
  You concentrate only on the primary conversion actions, which bring in the most profits. You do not acknowledge that the visitor could take mini-conversion steps, building up to the desired conversion. You neither measure these mini-conversion actions, nor do you make the effort to persuade your visitors to make the conversion.

If you checked *yes* to most, or all, of the above points, you are suffering from what is called the Greedy Marketer Syndrome.

As an extension of the furniture website spoken of earlier, if the primary aim of your visitors is to just look at the furniture designs on your website, but not buy, then it may seem you need not bother with marketing to them. After all, that is not what you want. *Exactly!* That is not what *you* want. *You* want them to *buy* from the website. *You* want them to trust you enough to spend their money on the products.

But, let's not forget the visitors' intent here.

As a marketer, it is tempting to focus on the hot (Definitely Yes) or warm (Slightly Yes) leads. The reason being they are easy to convince into taking the conversion action. Also, the success rate is high. One little push, and the leads will behave exactly the way you want them to.

TRUE CONNECTIONS

When a marketer thinks only of these leads and focuses all the energy into marketing to them, they are being greedy. They are simply acting out their selfish motives to make money quickly and easily.

If you have considerable traffic from visitors who come just to browse through your website and compare prices, make sure they get what they are looking for. Give them a good experience. Let the search process be simple and easy for them. The financial benefit from doing this may come later, or, it may not come at all. But you would have given the visitor a feel-good experience and you would have done your part in ensuring that when the visitor closes your webpage, they will do so with the satisfaction of accomplishing what they wanted. This is just one of the ways you can build a real connection with your visitors.

Websites make it difficult to perform simple tasks like searching for something, browsing through products, or reading the content manage to do only one thing: annoy visitors so much they remember not to visit the website again.

Care to know other advantages of knowing what the visitor wants and why you should cater to their needs?

1. Your customers feel secure when they see you offer exactly what they need. It reinforces the feeling of being in the right place.

2. Your goal of getting the customer to take the desired conversion action is met.

3. If your website ensures the customers have the best experience while carrying out the conversion action, it is going to add a lifetime value to those customers. After all, happy, satisfied customers are bound to come back to you for similar needs.

4. Happy customers who believe in you will willingly spread the word about your business. This could be reflected in social media shares, online reviews and ratings, and even word-of-mouth publicity.

Another disadvantage of the Greedy Marketer Syndrome is you get too used to the comfort zone and do not want to try anything new. This is really limiting to the potential your business has. Conversion Rate Optimization is not a one-time activity; it is a continuous process. If you're not willing to make changes to the way you work, and fine-tune your strategy continuously, you can't make a huge difference to how your website works.

You would be amazed at just how many Digital Marketers suffer from Greedy Marketer Syndrome. Just look at yourself. Now, even though this approach may work, it puts a limit on your website's success. You are probably achieving your sales target solely by sticking to a single tried and tested strategy but, you are giving up on the opportunity to build a relationship with new people.

Sometimes, there are visitors who are well within the boundaries of your target group, but they are not ready to take the ultimate leap of faith currently – that is, the desired conversion. If you choose to ignore these visitors, you are shouting from the rooftops you are just out for the "easy money" so you don't care about them. You are focusing on your goals and not really aligning those goals with those of some of the people in your target group simply because they aren't ready to commit to your business. You are basically not focusing enough on your *potential* customers' needs.

The cure for the syndrome is quite simple though – *Don't ignore the needs of all your visitors!* See? This is not rocket science.

As a marketer who wants to promote the brand as being trustworthy and credible, you must see what you can do to help all your visitors from the defined target group to take the conversion action. So, if you have visitors who come to your website but do not actually buy, don't ignore them. Instead, try to find out the reason behind the visitors bouncing off your website.

Are they doubtful about the quality of the furniture you offer? Build trust through *trust symbols* such as Better Business Bureau or Chamber of Commerce logos, awards won, customer testimonials, etc.

Do they think your checkout is too complicated and leave it mid-way? Declutter and simplify the process to make it more user-friendly.

Do they need more help deciding on the ideal piece of furniture? Suggest talking to your in-house experts or direct them to blogs on your website helping customers choose the furniture that's right for them.

While the questions could be endless, there are many ways to work out a solution. Let's look at the reason's visitors might hesitate to take the conversion action and ways to handle this in the subsequent chapters. For now, suffice to say it never is a good idea to ignore *any* of your visitors' needs.

With the right analytics tools, you can determine the bounce rate, but you can also determine at which stage the customers are bouncing. Being aware of the issues is the first step towards solving them. Getting more information on the issues is the second step.

What's Next?

By knowing the three important steps, you now have the formula for Digital Marketing success.

The ideal scenario is when your goals are perfectly aligned with what your website offers, which is perfectly in line with what your visitors are looking for.

The core of your marketing strategy should be to get this alignment right.

But, while you are at it, don't fall prey to Greedy Marketers' Syndrome!

THREE THINGS WEBSITE VISITORS ASK THEMSELVES

A few years ago, I was looking to buy some garden chairs. I saw one sponsored ad on Facebook for a website that caught my attention. The ad claimed to offer an introductory discount and it also had pictures of some nice-looking furniture. I thought the whole thing looked quite promising and decided to investigate this website further before buying from my *tried and tested* vendor.

As soon as I opened their homepage, I was lost. It took me quite a while to figure out where I was supposed to look for garden chairs, and when I finally managed to find them, I couldn't filter or sort the results. So, essentially, I was left with rows and columns of pictures of chairs that kept loading as I scrolled down. This wasn't very helpful at all. The only thing that stood out was the Introductory Discount icon that was displayed *everywhere* on the website. Frankly, the discount meant nothing to me unless I found what I wanted, which was the perfect garden chairs!

I gave up on the website rather quickly as it neither made me feel good about the company, nor helped me to meet my needs. Despite all the effort that might have been put into it, it was clearly a poorly designed website.

TRUE CONNECTIONS

The average customer looking for something in the digital world is bombarded with choices. The number of websites and the massive amount of information they provide is staggering! There is a lot to be offered, but the customer is pressed for time so, every time a visitor lands on a website, they immediately start to gauge whether the website is going to provide them what they are looking for. Usually this decision is made within seconds, however, if there is enough motivation, the visitor might stay a little longer. But, at each stage of the navigation process, the visitor is judging the website and, if at any point, the visitor has a bad feeling about it, they are going to close the page and look elsewhere.

So, how do you ensure the visitor coming to your website stays and converts? What is that elusive *trick of the trade* that you need to know in order to be a successful Digital Marketer? Often, the answer to seemingly difficult questions like these are extremely simple.

You need to understand how your customers think! After all, a real connection with the customers comes only after a real understanding of them.

I have been saying this right from the beginning of this book: to be successful at Digital Marketing, you need to understand you can't only think of your selfish interests. You need to take care of the customers' needs, too. I cannot stress this point enough. You must absolutely take a real interest in your visitors, leads, and customers if you want to make a difference in your Digital Marketing.

It doesn't matter how much money you have spent generating traffic for your website. You still have mere seconds to convince visitors to stay. If you can't make an impression on them in the first few seconds, all it takes is *one click, and they're gone!*

As said earlier, the visitor is judging your website from the moment they land on your page. Currently, you aren't even talking about the quality of the products or services you have to offer. Let's go back to the furniture website experience. I'll give them the benefit of doubt they probably had good quality furniture at great discounts. But here, you are talking about how the website makes your visitors *feel*. For example, I felt neglected. I did not feel the website had any interest in me at all. I felt lost in the number of things they had to offer, and the website didn't provide me with any worth whatsoever.

So, what do visitors need?

The visitors who come to your website have probably seen a lot of similar websites before coming to you. They are probably already tired of looking at options and don't have all day. *The pressure to impress is real!*

Let's break down the thought process of a new visitor. Typically, at a subconscious level, your average visitor is looking to answer three important questions:

1. Am I in the right place?
2. How do I feel about this site?
3. What am I supposed to do here?

If your website can give visitors positive answers to these three questions, you get a *huge* advantage over your competitors. The visitors not only choose to stay on your website, the good experience also conditions them to be ready to go from visitor to customer.

If, on the other hand, the website fails to provide satisfactory answers to these questions, the visitors quickly lose interest. If they feel coming to the website is not worthwhile, they will not stay long, and there certainly will be no conversions coming your way.

The Three Questions

Now, let's see how you can help visitors get positive answers to the three important questions, so they choose to stay and explore further.

Am I in the Right Place?

This is the first question any visitor would be asking themselves. In the absolute chaos of websites vying with each other to prove they have exactly what the customer is looking for, your website visitor is usually wary. But look at the bright side – they're here, aren't they? Make the most of it. Here is what you can do:

Give Them What They're Looking For

This is more important than you'd think. Maybe your SEO content helped you get a visitor. Now, make sure you deliver what you promised in the snippet on the search engine results page. If you lead your visitors to believe they have finally found a website that has exactly what they need, but when they click on it, they realize it was only a mirage, they will be put off. If you do that, be assured they are going to avoid your website altogether during any subsequent searches.

The solution lies in designing excellent landing pages or microsites.

So, if a visitor comes to your website due to the promise of a free download, make sure you give them the download.

If a visitor comes to your page looking for black training shoes, make sure you take them to the exact page showing them black training shoes.

If a visitor comes to your blog, make sure you have great content.

Basically, remember that the visitors come with *their* selfish interest in mind and a timer in their hands. So, give them what you promised, and give it to them quickly.

The Value Plan

When people visit a website, they are only interested in one thing: what can the website offer them? Therefore, you need to have a strong value plan for visitors. A good value plan explains:

1. What the website provides the visitors
2. What unique benefit can the customers expect
3. How the website can help the customers fulfil their unique need
4. Why the customer should choose this website over others

A value plan is not about self-praise. Immediately after landing on your website, more than anything else, the visitor is interested in knowing what you can do for them. So, show them exactly that.

The Differentiating Factor

What is it that differentiates you from other websites offering the same products or services? If visitors can see the differences early on, they may feel they have finally come to the right place. It could be an industry-specific award, or it could be a considerable loyal customer base. But remember, this initial stage is not where you should be continually bragging about the company's achievements. It is only about making the visitor subtly aware of them. So, instead of lengthy pieces of content describing your accomplishments, a better idea would be to have a short line below your company logo. You can also create badges with the award names and place them on the webpage. However, don't go overboard by crowding the homepage with a badge for every little achievement. Select and highlight only one or two achievements which you think will have the most impact on visitors. For everything else, you could always have a separate link, which visitors can check if they want.

Use Your Telephone Number

Most people don't trust every website they come across, especially when it's about spending money or giving personal information. So obviously, when they come to a website, they are looking for things that help them decide if they can trust the business.

A telephone number, at the top right corner of your website is a huge trust symbol for visitors. Having a telephone number takes the digital element off the visitors' experience. It tells them they are dealing with real people who can be reached by telephone. With a telephone number, they know they can speak with someone *human* if they feel the need.

Build Trust - Social Proof

If you already have quite a few satisfied customers, this could be a good symbol of trust for new visitors. You can either display the number of customers prominently, or you could create a badge and place it with your other badges. This gives people a sense of security to know there are others who have spent money on or in some way benefited from offerings on your website.

When your existing customers have great things to say about you, make sure new visitors have access to the testimonials. You can insert a link to the customer reviews under a friendly phrase like "See what our customers say about this product". Knowing real people have already used and liked the products they are considering buying is a great trust booster. It helps the visitors make an informed choice. They feel more confident about what they are getting and what to expect. This assurance forms the basis of their trust when it comes to spending money on your business.

A few trust symbols placed on the homepage or landing page can help develop that initial level of trust. When the visitor is still asking themselves if they are in the right place, you need to give them a quick reassurance your website is trustworthy.

The webpage of *goldenfrog.com* is a perfect example of trust. The simple design quickly draws the eye to the fact that the website has provided their VPN services to over a million users. A few testimonials from existing customers builds trust even further.

Website hosting company Bluehost's homepage quickly earns the trust of visitors by letting them know it powers "over 2 million websites worldwide" and lets visitors know about their money-back guarantee the moment they land on the page.

Make Them Familiar with Your Business

If you have an *About Us* page, use it wisely. Don't just put routine details about your business. Make the content engaging and interactive. If visitors happen to click on the *About Us* link, make sure they really get to know your passion for the business and the driving force behind it. Tell them your story. Your business appears more trustworthy when visitors get to know the story of its inception, the story of its founders, etc. It helps forge a connection. They feel they know you, so trust comes easily.

Little Things Make a Big Difference

Trust symbols are necessary and effective, but these symbols alone can't help you. You need to make constant assurances, so visitors feel they are at the right place. A few things you could do to achieve this are:

- Show a visitor upfront you have what they are looking for. This means if a search for *blue leather handbags* led them to your website, make sure the landing page displays *blue leather handbags*.

- Do you think your line of business is inherently complex where the visitors need a lot of clarity before taking the conversion action? Help them in the decision-making process. Stay with them. Direct them to your FAQ page or to well-written blogs which might help them. If you think it would help, encourage them to speak with your experts on the telephone or through chat. These experts will help alleviate their doubts. This ensures any concerns your visitors might have are lessened at an early stage, so they are ready for the actual conversion.

- Whenever money is involved, be transparent. Tell the visitors exactly how much they need to spend while also letting them know it's a bargain. But, do not surprise them with hidden costs when they are making the actual payment. A customer would view that as a breach in trust.

- Is someone well-known endorsing your brand? Have their picture, along with a short quote about what they think about your business. This can be placed on the landing page to inspire new leads.

Again, remember not all your leads are the same. Know the temperature of your leads and design customized landing pages for each different type. Yes, it takes some effort, but the results are usually quite rewarding. A customized landing can make all the difference when it comes to answering the question "Am I in the right place?".

How Do I Feel About This Site?

When visitors are reassured, they have reached a website they can trust, the next question they ask themselves is "How do I feel about this website?". This is where having a good website experience comes into the picture. But what exactly is a good website experience? Well, it really is a broad term but, if you manage to make your visitors feel good about your website, they spend time browsing through it, so, you have a winner! A simple way to check this is to look at your bounce rate.

Giving a good website experience would depend largely on the type of business the website is built for. However, there are a few things that apply to all websites in general:

1. **The color schemes**
   No matter what you may think, it is always a bad idea to use too many colors on your website. Use subtle colors that are pleasing to the eye. Do NOT use colors that are so bright they blind your visitors! Stick to a color palette and be consistent in your color scheme.

2. **Pages that load quickly**
   If your web pages load slowly, even though they are impressive, you will have disappointed visitors who are closing the webpage and going to your competitors. In this era of instant gratification, you must optimize the website so the pages load quickly.

3. **Get rid of any distractions**
   When visitors are beginning to experience the website, you need to avoid things that would distract them. This includes moving banners, flash animation, sudden pop-ups, etc. You cannot expect visitors to like the website if they're not allowed to browse in peace.

4. **Make entering information easy for visitors**

   You want visitors to do more than just look at your website. You want them to complete subscription forms and enter personal details or payment information. If you want them to take these actions, it is only fair you make it as easy for them as possible. A few things you could do are:

   - Mark all mandatory fields with an asterisk (*). Clearly indicate all fields marked with an asterisk are mandatory. It would also be useful to tell them why you need this information.

   - When you require a date to be entered, clearly mention the format you need it in (example: mm/dd/yy). To make it even easier, you can provide individual boxes with dropdowns to enter the day, month, and year.

   - When you require the address, have separate fields for country, city, state/providence, etc. Use dropdowns wherever possible. This way, there is less of a chance of typing errors. It also saves the visitor from typing too much.

   - When using coupon codes, give visitors an option to look at all the available codes and let them choose the relevant one.

   - If you have sent out an email or a text message with a discount code along with the link to your website, it is a good idea to have the coupon code auto-fill when they click on the link from the email or text. This is more convenient than making them manually re-enter the coupon code when they get to the website.

5. **Be friendly, and be human**

   Visitors to your website should be treated as guests. Be friendly to them. Even when you make it very easy for visitors to enter information, there are some who will make mistakes when typing into the search bar, when entering a coupon code, or while filling out a form. The last thing you want to do is to blame them for it so, avoid impersonal messages just show an error has occurred, but aren't very helpful in explaining what was wrong and how to fix it. *The coupon code you have entered seems invalid. Please check again* sounds much better than an impersonal *Invalid data entered*. It makes the visitor feel they are dealing with real people instead of machines.

The first step towards making your visitors feel at ease is to talk to them like a human, not a computer, when they make mistakes. The simplest way to do this is to not rely on the programmer to write the error messages for you.

6. **Make searching easier**
   When visitors want to search for something on your website, make it easy and efficient for them. If you have an internal search engine, it should accommodate any typing errors. Having an accurate auto-suggest feature is extremely helpful for visitors. If that's not possible, a simpler way would be to monitor the search strings and look for the top 500 commonly mistyped words and set up featured results for these words.

7. **Use videos well**
   If you are using videos on your website as demonstrations, or to show testimonials from existing customers, make sure you use them well. Videos that start automatically are a big NO. They are distracting and could annoy a visitor. Videos posted without a short description are also a bad idea. Ideally, videos should be labeled with information about how long they are and what they are about. This allows visitors to decide whether they want to watch it.

8. **Make your visitors feel comfortable**
   When you ask visitors to give their personal information, make sure you tell them upfront how the information will be used by you. Will you use their email address to send them newsletters or to send them details on the latest products? Whatever it is, if

they're going to trust you with their personal information, make sure they know exactly what they are signing up for.

9. **Don't abandon your customers after they have paid!**
   This is the worst marketing faux pas you could commit. If you feel your work is done and you can move on once a customer spends money on your business, you are wrong. You need to thank them for trusting you. If they bought a product from you, give them the details necessary allowing them to track their package. This could be done by redirecting them to a landing page after the purchase is completed, or by sending a follow-up email. Basically, don't let visitors feel you no longer value them after they complete a purchase.

10. **Use animations with caution**
    We said above you don't need videos and other animations on your website if you don't want to distract your visitors. But, if you think animations and videos are necessary and effective in your marketing strategy, use them. But use them wisely. Animations that freeze up all the time can't be good for any website. Also, if your animation comes with background music, don't start the music without warning so visitors will know to turn their sound on or off.

What Am I Supposed to Do Here?

When a visitor is convinced your website is the right place and they feel good about it, that is the perfect moment to lead them to the conversion action. Ideally, your website should have a clear Call to Action (CTA).

If visitors come to your website to make a purchase, they should be able to easily find the pages with the images of the products. If visitors come to you for a download, they should be able to quickly figure out how to start the download. If they come for a webinar, they should be able to find it quickly and the session should launch without any difficulty.

TRUE CONNECTIONS

That brings you to the rules to follow in order to help the visitor answer the third question.

1. **Rules for CTAs**

    <u>Clearly Visible CTA</u>

    The problem here is website owners get self-absorbed instead of thinking of their visitors. They will show visitors what THEY want the visitors to see rather than let the VISITOR decide what they want to see. Visitors don't want to look at your website just to appreciate the clever design. They want their needs met quickly and efficiently. They would prefer if everything is brought to them neatly and served on a platter. If this doesn't happen, visitors will lose interest and move on instead of taking the time to look through the site

    <u>Distinct CTAs</u>

    If you have multiple CTAs, make sure your visitors are not confused about where they are supposed to click.

    - Wherever possible, visitors should be presented with a CTA relevant to them.

        For example, if you offer different products for personal use and for business use, you should have different CTAs depending on the visitor's needs.

    - If all visitors are directed to the same page, give them a clear idea about which CTA is relevant to them.

        For example, give buyers a choice based on whether they are looking for men's or women's clothing. Make the distinction easy to spot by highlighting in pink or blue. Remember vagueness and confusion will cause customers to doubt you.

This little doubt can make all the difference between someone responding to the CTA or ignoring it.

Prominent and consistent buttons

All buttons such as *Submit, Next, Register*, etc. should be easily visible. They should stand out, but they shouldn't be too loud. They should also be consistent, i.e., they should have the same color, font, and format throughout your website. For example, all "Next Page" buttons should have the same format, all *Buy Now* buttons should be same, etc. This consistency means that when a user has spent a considerable amount of time on your website, they know on sight which button means what, without having to read the text on the button. When users have this level of comfort while browsing through your website, their trust for you goes up. They find navigation on your website easy so taking the desired conversion action comes more naturally to them.

Persistent CTAs when needed

When you have a website that has a lot of information on its pages, your CTAs must be repeated several times. The information could be only text or a combination of text, images, videos, etc., but, in any case, if the user must scroll down the page several times to get to the bottom, then have CTAs at regular intervals. The CTA should be a button that is hard-to-miss, preceded by content designed to influence the customer to act. But, if the visitor is reading through your content, nearing the end, and still not willing to act, you need to make a last-ditch attempt to persuade them. It could be a short, insistent message accompanying the CTA button such as "Hurry! Only a few seats remaining!!", or "Last day to take advantage of this offer!", or "Register today to receive a 10% discount", or something similar. These messages usually bring about a sense of urgency in the minds of customers. If you succeed in convincing them it's now or never, or they might be losing out on a good deal if they procrastinate in taking action, it might be just the push they need and you might just get the conversion you wanted.

Thoughtful CTAs

Make sure your CTAs are crystal clear. This includes designing each CTA button, so they are uniform in color and size. You must also make sure visitors know exactly what they are going to get when they click on these buttons. Always remember, a little bit of positivity goes a long way! So, for example, if you are collecting their personal information for a webinar registration, instead of having the regular *Submit* button at the end, you could have something that says, "I am ready to know more!" If a visitor is browsing through the various products you have, instead of an impersonal *Next* button for accessing more products, something that says "Show me more products" seems more personal. The idea behind this is to keep the visitor excited and upbeat about the whole process by showing your enthusiasm.

2. **Use pop-up windows to your advantage**
   Pop-up windows can be used when customers look like they are lost and are about to leave. When you feel the visitor is ready to leave your webpage without taking a conversion action, you could use pop-up messages as a last resort to help you save a lead. It could be a simple message such as "Are you sure you want to leave? Explore more NOW!", or "Still confused? Chat with our experts!", or "Did not find what you are looking for? Tell us about it". Basically, what you want to do here is just make the visitors trust you a little more, so they feel inclined to stay on the page a little longer. A few more seconds on your page can make all the difference, if this time is used wisely. So, if you are asking them to stay when they really want to move on, make sure you make it up to them. Either offer them a good deal, help them in their decision making, or ask for their feedback if they aren't satisfied, thank them for taking their time to give feedback, and promise to do better next time.

3. **Don't make visitors think too much**

    Every time you make your visitors think too much, they lose interest in staying on your website. Assume people who come to your website do not like to think at all. The looser ends you leave, the more they are going to be forced to think. Instead, offer solutions. Offer enough content to help them decide and be with them throughout the decision-making process right up to the conversion.

    If you make visitors think too much about how to take the conversion action, you might be losing a valuable lead or even a potential customer. Assume your visitors are eternally tired people who have absolutely no energy left to test their memory. So wherever possible, don't make them remember things. Every time you make your visitors think, they lose interest.

    - When they have filtered search results, clearly display what filters they have used, so they don't need to remember it.

    - When users have already looked at some links on your website, show these links in a slightly different color so they don't have to remember which parts they have already browsed.

    - Use the same font, format, and color for the same buttons such as *Submit, Next*, and other CTAs on each page. This helps visitors quickly distinguish the buttons without having to think too much about it.

    - If you have a website that sells products customers buy regularly, such as cosmetics, grocery items, etc., save their previous purchases. Once a visitor signs in, show them the link to their previous purchases so they can easily select the things they need without having to go through the search process again. The same applies to websites delivering food. The customers should have an option to repeat an order they have previously received without having to go through the selection and customization process again.

- If a visitor lands on your website using a referral code provided by a repeat customer, acknowledge the referral. A thank-you note to the customer who referred the lead is also a good idea. If it's a coupon code from an affiliate, say something positive about the affiliate. It not only adds a personal touch, but also helps establish trust in your business. It helps to make the visitors identify with your website and your business as something real.

People love comparing

When it comes to buying, customers obviously want the best deal for themselves. They want to know what the competitor website is offering in terms of price, features, add-ons, etc. If a feature of your product or service compares better than others, find a way to tell this to your visitor without putting down your competitor. A good way to do this is to reference a website offering comparisons between products. Let the visitors know how your product or service ranks according to that website.

4. **Make the content easy to scan**

   Visitors won't usually read all your content, but they will scan it. Of course, exceptions are blog sites, white papers, or academic content published on your websites. If you remember this, you will understand the futility of having lengthy, monotonous content on your website. Most visitors will simply glance at it and skim through the content.

   It's best to do away with lengthy content on your website entirely and save it for your blogs. However, even then, make the content modular. Use sub-headings, bullet points, numbered lists, and infographics. This increases the chances of visitors actively going through the content. If you have enough sub-headings, visitors can choose to read only the parts they find relevant to their needs.

5. **Help them all the way**
   When you have done everything you could, and your visitor is convinced to take the conversion action, make sure you help them at every step during the conversion.

   Make sure the content you expose the visitor to isn't vague. Stay away from fine print and be clear, concise and transparent.

   For instance, if your lead is ready to make a high value purchase from your website, make sure you help them in the following ways:

   - Clearly let them know how much their total order will be so they know how much they need to pay.

   - If you have a finance option, give the details clearly. If you need the customer to qualify for the financing option, help them provide you the correct details by telling them precisely what you need and why.

   - People are often possessive of their personal information. Tell them exactly how you will use their information and assure them it won't be misused.

   - Give them a clear timeline regarding when they will receive the product.

   - Once the product is shipped, provide them with a tracking number so they can track their purchase with the shipper.

   - Make sure they have the contact information for your helpline or customer care, so they can communicate with you, if necessary.

   - Encourage your customers to give feedback. The feedback could be about the product they purchased, as well as their buying experience. Always acknowledge the feedback. In case of criticism, apologize for the shortcomings in your process and assure them you take their comments seriously and are working to correct any inconsistencies.

If you're looking for lead generation from your traffic, or looking to expand your list of subscriptions, you may want to encourage the visitors to provide you with their necessary information. Also, simplifying the process so it is quick and easy will ensure visitors don't give up mid-way. Visitors will get frustrated if the subscription forms or surveys you make them take are too lengthy or difficult.

If your visitors mainly come to your website to research something, make sure your content is top notch. Help them by having an efficient internal search bar so they can get to the content they are looking for quickly.

Summary

If you succeed in establishing your reputation as a trustworthy business in the eyes of your website visitors, that is one of the most important things you could do towards fulfilling your goals. And, the best part is you also help the visitors realize they have reached a place where they can fulfil their goals too! A perfect alignment, wouldn't you say?

MARKETING TO THE TOP OF THE FUNNEL VS THE BOTTOM OF THE FUNNEL

A Sales Funnel (sometimes referred to as a Purchase Funnel), is the process through which a marketer leads their visitors towards the desired action, which is the purchase. The Sales Funnel has stages, and with each stage, the number of participants decreases until the last stage, where only those who are ready to go through with the purchase remain.

The most common Sales Funnel has four stages as defined by the well-known AIDA model for marketing and advertising. The four stages are Awareness, Interest, Desire, and Action.

Visitors drop out from each stage until ultimately, only those who are convinced to buy, remain. So, the funnel starts out with a greater number of visitors and by the final stage, only a part of the original number remains. Let's now look at each stage of the AIDA model in detail.

Awareness

Awareness is the first stage of the funnel and has the largest number of visitors. In this stage, the visitor is aware of what they need in order to find a solution to their problem or satisfy a need. They find the relevant category and search for a product or service. They now want to learn more about it in order to confirm it will be useful for them.

Don'ts of the Awareness Stage:

- **Banner ads** – Banner ads distract visitors and cause more harm than good. In the critical, initial moments of awareness, distractions must be kept at bay.

- **Entry popups** – Entry popups ruin the website experience to a great extent. If you must have popups, let them appear when the visitor is about to leave.

- **Cluttered homepages** – If you can't decide which are the most important products and/or services and want to include everything on the homepage, you get cluttered homepages. This leads to confusion and bad UX (User Experience).

Dos of the Awareness Stage

- Stop overwhelming your visitors with too much information that comes too soon and is too loud.

- Keep the choices to a minimum. You need to help visitors solve a problem, not add to their problem by giving them so many options they are left confused.

- Get rid of the clutter on your homepage as well as on subsequent pages. If you think something is important and must be on the homepage, think again. Test, remove, and test again until you are left with clear, uncluttered webpages. This makes only the important products/services stand out and increases the chances of visitors moving through the funnel to the next stage.

Rules of Awareness

- If a visitor can't find something on the website quickly enough, it does not exist for that visitor. Website browsing shouldn't be a quest to find hidden CTAs.

- Moderation is key. If you try to put the emphasis on too many qualities of your business, everything loses importance.

- Any delay in loading pages or returning search results, causes frustration and makes the website lose credibility.

Interest

This is the second state of the funnel. The number of visitors in the Interest Stage has dwindled since some visitors will have left the website at the Awareness Stage. Here, visitors display a certain level of interest in a specific category of product or service and are eager to research more. They want more information that will better explain the products/services in the category to them and give them a better idea of what to expect.

The Interest Stage has a lot of potential for interaction with the visitors. This is where you can lead them to navigate the website and explore all their options.

Rules for making the most of the Interest Stage:

- Understand who the customer is. Help them with role-based navigation at this stage so they will continue forward.

- Understand what the customer is trying to do. Identify their need for specific task completion and help them with task-based navigation in order to help them get closer to finding the solution they are looking for.

Desire

In the Desire Stage, which is the third stage of the funnel, the visitor has already determined what it is they need or desire. They are convinced they have found what they want, and they are almost ready to finalize the purchase. But first, they want to compare features, check for reliability, assess the pricing, etc., to ensure this really is the product or service they should purchase.

Activities typical to the Desire Stage are:

- Researching
- Comparing features or pricing
- Getting detailed information
- Customization (if applicable)

Rules for making the most of the Desire Stage:

- Make research worthwhile by providing easy-to-scan, good quality content.
- Eliminate frustration by giving them options if they reach a dead-end. Don't let the desire fizzle out.
- Make the visitor feel welcome and appreciated for using your website.
- Make them feel safe by giving them plenty of trust cues and being transparent in the information offered.
- Let visitors feel in control when they are browsing or taking any other action on the website.

Action

In the final, Action Stage, of the funnel, the customer is ready to complete the purchase. They have chosen the specific product they wish to buy as well as the specific source from which they want to buy it. All that is left is to enter their payment information.

During this stage, the top question in the visitor's mind is, *"Why should I buy from your website?"*.

If you can answer this question to the visitor's satisfaction, you have a successful sales funnel.

The key aspects to help visitors believe your website is the best place to buy from are:

- **Brand value** – The brand value is a huge driving force in making people buy from you. However, it takes time to build brand value. So, if your business isn't a known brand yet, there's a lot you need to do before you can use brand value to influence customers.

- **Previous experience** – If customers have previously made purchases from your website and they have had a good experience, they are more likely to trust you with their money again.

- **Total solution** – Are you able to provide customers with a total solution for their needs, or only a part of it? Customers would prefer to get the whole package from one source.

- **Risk free action** – The website should be able to dispel all doubts and fears from the customers' minds by providing complete transparency.

- **Establish credibility** – You need to establish your credibility through trust symbols, authoritative content, and other proofs. Whenever possible, use actual customer testimonials.

Rules for the Action Stage

- Don't get in the customer's way when they are moving towards completing their purchase. Stand back and let them finish. This is not the time to cross-sell, to ask for feedback or to have them fill out surveys.

- Make the process as easy and user-friendly as you possibly can. This means no mandatory sign-ups, no complicated check-outs, and do not let them search for what to do next.

- No surprises at the last minute! Don't spring hidden costs, shipping charges, or minimum order value requirements on the customer just when they are about to enter their payment information. Instead, make sure the customers have a complete idea of what the purchase will cost them BEFORE they proceed to the payment screen.

Remember at each stage, the number of visitors is going to be reduced. You cannot do much about that fact. That's the reason it's called a sales *funnel* and not a sales *barrel*. The output is going to be less than the input.

So how do you win at funneling?

- By ensuring a good input – a high number of people at the top of the funnel.

- By minimizing losses at each stage.

When you have traffic with different goals, you need different sales funnels for each of them. Funnel designing starts with mapping a visitor's journey from the first point of contact through the conversion.

The Top of the Funnel

The answer to a good start for the funnel is traffic. Marketers spend a lot of time and money to increase the number of website visitors using SEO for organic traffic, paid searches, PPC campaigns, engaging influencers and affiliates, social media campaigns, advertising, etc.

There are three aspects of traffic that need to be considered for an effective campaign:

1. The source of the traffic – Testing can reveal which source is getting you the most traffic, and which ones are yielding poor results.

2. The quality of the traffic – Are people just coming to your website from clickbait? That never ends well for anybody.

3. The intent of the traffic – What are visitors expecting to get when they come to your website?

Out of these three, the most important aspect of incoming traffic is intent. The more information you can have about the intent of the visitors, the easier it is for you to lead them all the way through the funnel.

It is a marketer's dream to get traffic that comes with the intent of converting. So, for an e-commerce site, the visitors might directly go to the product pages and quickly go through with the purchase. For a lead generation or subscription website, the visitors might readily give their contact information so someone can contact them through email or send them newsletters. The conversion rate in these cases goes through the roof. But in real life, this seldom happens. Customers are not always ready to hit the *Buy Now* or *Subscribe Now* button, so marketing to the top of the funnel requires specialized attention and strategy.

This kind of *Buy Now* or *Subscribe Now* marketing is completely targeted towards the bottom of the funnel. For some unknown reason, many websites assume all visitors are ready to buy. This does not cater to the needs of those visitors who are merely looking for information.

The correct way to market to the top of the funnel

The top of the funnel requires a good strategy and a good deal of patience. The visitors are usually in research mode at this stage. They need information that can make the decision-making process easier.

Instead of intruding on their personal space and asking for information, websites should be designed to provide high quality information to the visitors. The information could be in the form of a content-centric landing page, or separate downloadable files from which the visitors can choose the ones they need. After they are provided with free, valuable, high quality information, that is the time you earn the right to ask for something in return – in this case, their personal information so you can contact them.

By helping visitors access information on your website, you don't just prove to them you can provide value, you also get an excellent opportunity to understand what they are looking for by tracking their actions on the website. By looking at what content they are reading or downloading, you can send them specific promotional content instead of sending generic messages about products or offers.

Gaining traffic is a continuous process. Even when you have a sufficiently large pool of regular customers, your efforts to generate traffic shouldn't stop. If your efforts stop, you will be limiting your potential profits to a great extent. Also, no matter how large a pool is, if you don't add into it regularly, it is sure to dry up at some point.

However, all this doesn't mean you should try to trick people into coming to your website. If the visitors do not belong to your target group, or if you do not have what they need, the number of visitors just becomes a statistic that adds to your bounce rate, nothing more.

Ways to generate meaningful traffic:

- **SEO**
  Search Engine Optimization is the most used traffic generation method to improve organic traffic. But, choose and use keywords wisely. SEO is a complex concept, to say the least, and *keyword stuffing* is never the answer.

- **Social media**
  Social media has a lot of potential to attract motivated traffic. Due to the interactive nature of these platforms, it is a good place to understand user needs so they are presented with customized solutions, which will boost traffic.

- **PPC**
  Sponsored ads to get people to visit your site also work, if you deliver what you promise in the ad. These could be ads on the search engine's results page with good visibility. Well thought-out PPC campaigns can improve traffic drastically.

- **Influencers and affiliates**
  Influencers and affiliate programs can get traffic that is coming with a very powerful intent to convert. You can track the success and pay per each successful lead received to get the best out of affiliate programs.

- **Offline advertising and celebrity endorsements**
  Advertising through TV, newspapers, or magazines can also work depending on the audience you are aiming to impress. You can also build brand awareness through offline events, tradeshows, workshops, etc. Traffic from these sources is usually already motivated to actively explore your website.

- **Media-rich ads**
  Media-rich ads, such as animation or video ads, that run on other websites can also generate interest for users to visit your website.

- **Word of mouth publicity and customer referrals**
  When you have given a great buying experience to customers, they will be telling their friends about it. When this happens, you have traffic that comes with the expectation the website will be a good experience for them, too. Customers can also be encouraged to spread the word about your business by providing them with an incentive-based referral program.

- **Regularly updated content**
  Content that is regularly updated improves search result rankings. It also gives regular visitors value out of visiting your website. Once you have established your authority in a niche, readers will seek you out on their own every time they want information in that niche.

- **Email lists**
  Email lists are built using various sources:

  - **Renting from a third party to use their existing email list.** For example, the list can be customized to some degree based on your target demographic. However, this would come under the category of unsolicited emails, so the success rate could be low. But, if the open rate is good, you can at least hope for good brand recognition.

  - **Getting visitors to give their email addresses in exchange for attending a webinar or registering for an event.** In this case, the visitors have at least some idea of what they are getting into, and a marketing email from your company might have a better open rate.

  - **User registrations and subscriptions.** This is where users willingly seek out emails from you at a regular frequency. They already have a good enough reason to take an interest in your business.

- **Existing customers.** The most valuable people on your email lists are those who are existing customers. They have given you express permission to communicate with them, via email, to let them know more about your business, or about new products and offers.

  If you send relevant, useful information, and don't flood these customers' inboxes with repeat emails, you should receive a good response. Segmenting emails based on the type of recipients is quite effective in making sure the emails are relevant.

There will be visitors who encounter your brand, or even your website, that might not be ready to buy immediately. The idea behind a sales funnel is to acknowledge this and nurture the relationship with those visitors to help them to engage with the website.

Many times, the top of the funnel (awareness) is the first contact people have with your website. However, it could also be repeat visitors who haven't done anything besides casual browsing. It could also be visitors who come to your website often, but for some reason, do not take any action.

Here are some possible scenarios to consider when visitors are at the top of the funnel:

- **Curiosity about your business** – Visitors saw an ad about your business and want to look at your website.

- **Researching something specific** – Visitors know what they want. They are seeking information and are looking for good, quality content from a trustworthy source.

- **Searching for a specific product** – The visitors know what they need, but don't know whether the website has it. They want to search for the product in the categories. They also want to know more about the product.

- **Comparing before buying** – The visitors know what they need, and they know your website has it. They just want to get more details such as features, pricing, delivery timelines, reviews, etc., before taking that final step.

- **Specific intent to buy** – They have already decided they want to buy from your website. For them, it is just a matter of searching for the desired product or service and going ahead with the purchase.

Understanding user intent and aligning it with the website goals is what really improves the success of a funnel. Therefore, when you have different visitors, with different intents, the funnels might vary.

What Happens Inside the Funnel?

The number of visitors still present at the bottom of the funnel are those who contribute to your profits, and in order to keep this number high, you need to do everything right at each stage of the funnel.

In Digital Marketing, each of these funnel stages take place on the actual website. There is a lot of hype over traffic generation and customer retention, so, effort must be made at traffic generation where marketers leave no stone unturned in ensuring quality traffic finds its way to their website. They spend money to test which traffic sources work the best for them, and they constantly tweak their strategy to ensure a continuous flow of traffic.

Once traffic is generated, marketers move on to customer retention efforts. Now that everybody has acknowledged the benefits of having regular, paying customers, follow-up emails are promptly sent after a sale. Here is where attempts are made to cross-sell by offering discounts on related and future purchases. Every effort should be made to ensure the customers' continued association with the brand.

Sometimes, marketers tend to forget the actual conversions take place on the website. If not for the conversions, generating traffic is useless, and the efforts for customer retention are not justified.

Conversion Rate Optimization (CRO) is the percentage of visitors who take the conversion action. The following are the essential requisites:

1. You must understand what purpose you are trying to serve by creating the website.

2. You must understand who your target audience is.

3. You must understand the needs of the target audience.

4. You must know if the target audience is finding what they need.

We know every visitor is asking themselves three questions when they visit a website: *Am I in the right place? How do I feel about this site? What am I supposed to do here?*

A website with good CRO is the one that satisfactorily answers these three questions on every page of the website.

The Bottom of the Funnel

The primary goal of the bottom stage of the funnel is to have conversions. You can get the best out of this stage by maximizing the funnel performance by:

- Increasing order value, thereby increasing the monetary gains.

- Optimizing the customer experience so they leave the website happy and satisfied.

TRUE CONNECTIONS

Marketing does not end just because the purchase has been made. The customers who go through the last stage of the funnel still need your attention. This is the **Retention phase.**

Once the customers have purchased from you, you need to start efforts to retain their loyalty with your website. This involves:

- Post-purchase registration
- Good customer service
- Good packaging and timely delivery
- Follow up emails
- Carefully segmented emails to keep the customer interest alive
- Making it easy for customers to return to the website by giving incentives or loyalty bonuses
- Giving the customers some reason to check the website regularly, such as introducing exclusive offers on a regular basis
- Encourage customers to refer the website to their contacts

The good news is, that in this stage, the customer has already gained some familiarity with your website and marketers are very aware of the potential of getting the retention stage right. You are basically creating a loyal customer base who will keep coming back to you.

Instead of trying something completely new, people like the comfort of going through a tried and tested route.

Email Marketing According to the Funnel Stage

Top of the funnel

Typically, for the stages at the top of the funnel, your aim is to educate and create awareness about your brand, so the emails need to be content-oriented. Think newsletters, blog post links, invites for brand awareness events, webinars, etc. The idea is to familiarize the users with the business and give them information.

Even though you could have product recommendations or CTAs about making purchases, the focus should be on information, with the CTA presented very subtly, if at all, and always blended into the information.

For instance, if a website sells maternity clothing, but also publishes a blog on educating expectant and new mothers, the top of the funnel should be more about providing them with good content. However, within a blog post on how the body changes during pregnancy, and how the right maternity wear can provide comfort, you can provide a subtle CTA about the type of clothing you have on your website.

Bottom of the funnel

In the bottom stages of the funnel, the focus shifts away from information. The visitor knows enough about your brand. It's time to get them ready for action. This is where you move in for the kill, so to speak. Your content can now lean more towards promotion and sales, you can talk about your products and promotional offers and you can have very visible and easily actionable CTAs in the emails. If you are dealing with existing customers, you can cross-sell and encourage referrals.

Understanding the Funnel by Looking at Visit Stats

To move the visitor target group from the top of the funnel to the bottom, you can map their journey by looking at the number of visits they make. For example, say you have a website that deals in customized workbooks for children. If you are correctly tracking website visits, you will see some visitors regularly come to the website to read the informative blogs and free resource material. This indicates they are already in the Interest Stage of the funnel. To heighten their interest in the business, you could invite them to a webinar. If they decide to attend the webinar, it means they have now become very interested and are on the brink of the Desire Stage. With an introduction to the product and a little push and they should be ready to act.

PERSUASION

How often do you visit a website to buy something, but somewhere between browsing the products and buying something, you give up because you don't feel motivated enough, or comfortable enough to go through with the purchase? This behavior is apparent in the bounce rates and abandoned carts on any given website.

When people are coming to your website, but leaving without taking any action, it means you are not giving them enough reason to stay and act. You cannot just expect visitors to act in a certain way unless you make some effort to convince them that acting is going to help them. Remember the selfish goals of your visitors and how safeguarding their interests should be taken seriously? You need to convince visitors that a certain action taken by them can help them meet their goals. This action, in turn, would help fulfill YOUR business goals. Again, a proper alignment between the user's intent and your business goals would result in successful conversions.

The space between the point when a visitor lands on a website and the point when they make the conversion is the space where persuasion must occur.

So, what exactly is persuasion?

Persuasion is a skill, a technique, a strategy, and an art all rolled into one. It is largely based on understanding the psychology, behavior, motivations, and needs of a person in order to influence their choices.

Let's take the example of someone who smokes a pack of cigarettes a day. If you tell them to quit smoking because it is harmful to their health, you are just stating fact. But, if you want to *persuade* them to quit smoking, you will need to change their *attitude* towards smoking.

Similarly, imagine a child who goes to school and gets homework every day. This child does not particularly like doing homework, but if the parents and the teachers tell the child to do the homework because *they must do it*, that isn't persuading them to do it. The child would do it out of obligation, but that doesn't mean they are doing it by choice. If, on the other hand, the child is given reasons and proofs so they can understand why doing the homework is important, and given incentives and encouragement, their attitude towards homework would change. It could then be said they were *persuaded* to do the homework.

Persuasion is multi-layered. It's not aimed at simply telling someone what to do; it is all about giving someone enough reason to *choose* to do it themselves. There is a world of difference between telling someone what to do and *persuading* them to do it. Today's consumers are much too smart to buy something just because you tell them to buy it.

When a person is presented with a piece of information targeted at persuading them to take a conversion action, there are two ways in which that person can think:

1. The person might analyze all the information presented and then make the decision to act. This involves a considerable amount of thought.

2. The person might make an impulsive decision without giving the information too much thought. They might scan through the

information presented, but instead of analyzing it, they are ready to take whatever is presented to them at face value.

How the person is thinking at any given point in time depends on a lot of factors such as how significant they see the information, their emotional state at that point, and what they think is at stake. Persuasion in marketing obviously gets easier if you can get the person to decide without thinking too much. The key here is to reduce cognitive friction as much as possible. There are many ways to do this, which will be discussed in this chapter. However, let's clarify this does not mean you can't hope to persuade people who are thoroughly analyzing your information.

So, why do you think a person would choose to do something? Everybody is selfish so, it follows if you succeed in making people think doing something is beneficial to them, they are likely to *choose* to do it. When your persuasion appeals to the self-interest of the users, they could really be convinced.

Need for Persuasion

Let's take the example of Ms. A., who is the Wealth Management expert for a well-known bank. She handles the accounts of individuals with a high net worth and makes near-perfect decisions on investments while often taking calculated risks. Her clients are quite impressed by her knowledge and expertise, and they trust her choices. But, if you leave Ms. A. in a store where she is supposed to buy clothing for herself, it's a disaster! She can't seem to find anything suitable to wear even after hours of walking up and down aisles full of clothes. Then, after an eternity, when she does find the right outfit, she can't decide which shoes would go with it! The whole ordeal of deciding on an outfit and then choosing the accessories to go with it is so tiring and time-consuming for her, that she tends to avoid going shopping altogether. That is, until she hires the services of a personal shopper at the store. The personal shopper picks out only the things that are specific to Ms. A.'s current shopping needs and helps her choose from a small quantity of carefully selected outfits. The personal shopper also gives

Ms. A. advice on what looks good on her and helps make her shopping experience quick and productive.

So, why does a woman who is a confident decision maker at the workplace fumble when it comes to shopping? It is quite normal for people who are known to display certain qualities in one situation to be completely different in another situation.

The point to note here is that Ms. A., who is known for the quick decisions she makes while at work, is as indecisive as it gets when it comes to shopping. Without someone to help her choose clothes, she would be lost!

The same thing is happening with your website visitors. Without a little bit of handholding, they are probably lost in the maze of your webpages. Not all visitors have the motivation and patience to wade through this maze and take the conversion action all by themselves. Most visitors would need guidance, and quite a bit of *persuasion*, to go ahead with the conversion – no matter how small these conversions are.

Incorrect Persuasion

It's not as if Digital Marketers do not understand the importance of persuasion. They are aware persuasion is at the heart of most conversions. So, what do they do? They immediately begin trying to persuade visitors as soon as they land on the website. They go all out and end up overdoing it, which only leads to high bounce rates and cart abandonments.

Examples of incorrect persuasion:

1. Websites trying to grab users' attention by showing them insanely insistent CTAs (such as *Buy Now!* or *Offer Ends Today!*), which keep flashing or popping up without warning.

2. Using empty, unnecessary, and often unfounded adjectives like *world-class, best in the industry, amazing benefits*, etc., to describe their products or services.

3. Popup windows that appear too soon to help.

4. Content that is meant to be persuasive but is just very long text that doesn't provide any value to the visitor.

5. Pointing the visitors towards products they are not looking for or interested in.

Have You Earned the Right to Persuade?

Yes, you want that conversion, but before you even think about using persuasion on a visitor, ask yourself these questions:

- Have you established enough trust?

- Have you given them enough information to make the decision to act?

- Have you proven yourself to be a credible source of the information you provide?

If you have answered NO to any of the above questions, clearly you haven't earned the right to ask anything of your visitors. First, you must earn the right to persuade!

Remember you cannot persuade anyone against their will. Maybe, what you have to offer is truly amazing but, if the user is not in a receptive frame of mind, you may as well be directing your persuasion efforts to a brick wall. The visitor can be persuaded only if you succeed in establishing trust, giving them valuable information, and proving your credibility.

Types of Conversions

There are two types of conversions:

1. **Conversions that require less time to decide**
   Some decisions are easily made. If a business can build a reasonable level of trust, visitors find it easy to make these decisions and take the conversion action. Examples of easy decisions are:

   - Sharing personal details by registering on a website.

   - Completing a survey on a website.

   - Rating the website experience.

   - Subscribing for a free newsletter.

   - Downloading a free white paper.

   - Purchasing an inexpensive item.

   - Purchasing items that are used regularly, such as groceries or cosmetics.

   - Providing a phone number or email address so the business can contact them with special offers, discounts or newsletters.

   Decisions like these require only a little motivation so there is less effort needed to persuade the visitor.

2. **Conversions that require more time to decide**
   Some conversion decisions require more thought on the part of visitors, and therefore, require more time. Examples of such conversion actions are:

   - Purchasing a high value item.

- Signing up for paid webinars or online training which would span over several months.

- Applying for admission to a trade school or university.

- Purchasing a product that is not immediately needed.

In these cases, the level of commitment required is high. The visitors might take more time because:

- They need more time to think about the purchase.

- They have a limited budget.

- They want to compare your product or service with similar offerings on the market.

- They are not able to make the decision on their own. In this case, they want to discuss the decision with someone else – a spouse, a friend, a work colleague, etc.

- They are not convinced they are getting a good deal.

- They need more information to make the decision.

- They do not have an immediate need and are only looking at the website for something they may need at a future date.

These decisions require more of the visitor's time and they require more persuasion from the marketer. Since it could be days, or even weeks, from the time the visitor comes to your website until the time they make the conversion, you need to use persuasion, but you also need patience.

Sometimes, people need help in understanding exactly what will fulfill their need. Once they know what they need, they must be persuaded into buying it from you. As a marketer, you need to identify the areas of doubt your visitors have and then work on clearing their doubts. Help them get clarity in their decision and that will help them to take the conversion action.

However, the transition from having a need be met to meet the need from your business, needs to be smooth and seamless.

The Subtle Art of Persuasion

Yes, persuasion is vital, but what good is persuasion if it infringes on another's personal space? A subtle, clear, and non-intrusive strategy is required to make the persuasion effective.

Subtle – Don't hound people with over-the-top persuasion. That is like a salesperson following a customer around a store trying to get them to buy an item. What usually happens is people leave the store without buying. You can expect similar results on a website.

Clear – Be clear on what you want to persuade a visitor to do and work only on that. Make sure the visitor also understands what you are asking of them – don't let there be any room for doubt.

Non-intrusive – Make sure you do not infringe on the visitors' personal space while persuading them. Let them feel in control and let them have enough space to make the decision by themselves.

Identify the Persuasion Need

Identify the persuasion needed for each visitor.

- Hot leads with enough motivation for conversion require minimal persuasion. It is more of a reassurance that their trust in your business is justified. If they are first time visitors coming from a strong referral, they need to feel their expectations of your website are being fulfilled.

Don't make the mistake of thinking hot leads do not require any persuasion at all. Sure, in most cases, they will convert. They might even overlook bad website design and annoying pop-ups to buy their favorite products from your website. They clearly have the motivation to persist and convert but, making the process easy for them and giving them incentives for their perseverance and loyalty is also a form of persuasion. You are basically persuading them to remain loyal to your business even if a worthwhile alternative is presented to them.

- Cold leads might never convert. These are the people who have no intention of buying from you and you probably can't convince them to convert even if you present the conversion action served on a platter. In other words, your effort to persuade them is wasted here but, they can be given enough proof of your credibility. This means when they have an urgent requirement for something you offer, they'll know where to go.

- The most opportunity for persuasion is the warm leads, which is also the largest pool of leads your business has. This is the area where your major persuasion efforts must be focused. Even if the warm leads lack a very strong motivation to make the conversion, they are still interested in your business and have the willingness to explore more. They also give you a reasonable chance to convince them to make the purchase. The high number of warm leads also means that when you succeed in convincing them, the number of conversions you can hope to get will be quite rewarding.

Identify the Right Time for Persuasion

Timing is everything when it comes to persuasion. Too soon and you seem pushy. Too late and the opportunity is lost. Visitors to your website may not always respond positively to persuasion efforts. Rather, you need to look for signs that it is the right time to persuade them.

TRUE CONNECTIONS

In his book *How to Win Friends and Influence People,* Dale Carnegie puts forth a very important principle. He says, "Get the other person saying 'yes, yes' immediately."

When you think about it, it's a very interesting concept. When someone says *No* in the beginning of an interaction, they are in the mental state to reject everything else that follows. When they enter this negative attitude mode, it becomes very difficult to bring them around to accept anything you want to share. However, when you get someone to say *Yes* outright, they are in a more forward-moving, accepting, and positive attitude.

Simply put, this means that for persuasion to work, the visitor must be in a positive frame of mind. This makes persuasion not only easy, but also more effective.

Now, how do you ensure your website visitor is in a positive state of mind?

I wish there was any easy answer to this question. A lot of factors go into determining the visitor's state of mind. Some of these factors are beyond your control. For example, if a person had an argument with their significant other before coming to your website, there's little you can do about that. You can't expect everybody to come to your website with a smiling face because that hardly ever happens. But you can eliminate any negative attitude towards *your website* by keeping the user's needs in mind.

If a visitor appears agreeable to everything they encounter on your website, they are more likely to take the conversion action when they come across it. If a visitor disagrees with whatever they see, they might: a) leave the website, or b) need some very strong motivation to continue. If a visitor has a neutral reaction, you still can use your power of persuasion!

Principles of Persuasion

1. **The Principle of Reciprocity**
Simply put, this principle, which is one of the Six Principles of Influence explained by Cialdini, relies on the human tendency

to reciprocate goodwill. If you give something to a person, they feel they should give you something in return. People are wired this way. They don't want to accept a favor without reciprocating.

When you apply this principle to marketing, if you give consumers something for free, they feel more inclined to do something for you – aka conversion.

For example:

- Give them some free, but useful content like a free webinar, a whitepaper, or a video tutorial.

- The best thing you can give people is your time. So, if it is relevant to your business, give them a free consultation.

- Give them free gifts or product samples.

- For return customers, you can give the gift of genuine, heartfelt appreciation. For instance, if you give them a discount coupon, they will be happy. But, if you give them a discount coupon with a personalized Thank You note that acknowledges their role in making your business grow, they will be even happier!

What you can expect in return is the customers' willingness to do something for you. If you want them to subscribe to your newsletter, they'll be more than happy to do it! If you suggest they try a new product, they'll be willing to pay for it! When you explain to them what more to expect from a paid consultation, they will be eager to sign up for it!

Counting on people to reciprocate for something you do for them is one of the simplest forms of persuasion. And it usually works!

2. **The Frequency of Illusion Principle**
   How often do you think about something and then you start to see it everywhere around you? Let's say you decide to get married.

TRUE CONNECTIONS

Suddenly, everyone around you is getting married or engaged. Right after you discover you are expecting a baby, you see babies and toddlers everywhere! Magical, isn't it? No, it's just psychology.

This sudden increase in the frequency of seeing something is an illusion. It is caused by *selective attention* sparked by an awareness of something new. It gives you the impression this new object or idea is suddenly everywhere.

This principle can be used in marketing by sending targeted information in order to condition the visitor. It involves tracking the online behavior and purchases of visitors, then, in a carefully planned manner, sending them information about something else you are selling. So, you send the visitor an email about a new, revolutionary product that just launched on your website. While browsing the Internet, the visitor sees the same product advertised. By the time the visitor sees a Facebook page sharing a positive review of this product, the visitor is convinced this product has merit and goes to your page to find out how to buy it.

3. **The Anchoring Principle**
People are always comparing things against a standard. They might not desire to drive the best car in the world, but they might ask themselves whether they have a better car than a friend, relative or co-worker.

Similarly, someone may be reluctant to buy something for $100, if they think the price isn't reasonable. But, if they believe the actual price is $180 and it's being offered for $100, they will jump at it.

Anchoring is hardly a new concept in Digital Marketing. Many websites use it to persuade the customers into buying something they would otherwise find overpriced.

4. **The Principle of Social Proof**
Nothing stirs the will to act in people like the knowledge others are acting too! It might seem a little harsh, but the world is full of

sheep with the *herd* mindset. If everybody around you is raving about the latest TV show, you feel you *must* watch it. If all your friends talk about reading and loving a new book, you can't wait to read it, too.

In marketing, when people are provided with proof that many other people are also subscribing, registering, buying, enrolling, etc., it stimulates the need in them to do the same.

For example, YouTube displays the number of subscribers for a channel. This is proof there are a lot of people who like this channel. This is a cue for a new consumer to jump on the bandwagon and subscribe.

You can use the power of numbers to persuade users to take a certain action.

Another way to demonstrate many others are buying a product is to display the number of people who have purchased the product, right next to the product description. Or, a banner on the homepage, which mentions the number of satisfied customers who have bought a product or used a service from the website also works.

Look at how *Hotels.com* shows information about a selected hotel. The room looks good in the pictures, the ratings are great, and the amenities are adequate. So far so good. But, if the visitor still has a slight hesitation before going ahead with the booking, a helpful pop-up informs them that reservations have been made at this hotel 14 times during the last 24 hours alone. That is immediate social proof others are not only interested; they are also booking rooms.

Showing social media *Shares* also has the same effect. When users see proof that many others have shared some content from a website on social media, it is an instant boost to the brand image. What's more, there is a good chance they, too, will share the page on social media. However, you don't want to create a negative social image. If the number of shares is low, it is better to wait for a respectable number before broadcasting it on the webpage.

5. **The Principle of Benefits**

    People are driven by self-interest. If they feel they will benefit significantly from a particular action, they will find the motivation to do it. If you tell a very busy person there is a hidden treasure in their backyard, they will take some time off and spend hours digging.

    In marketing, when you lead visitors to the conversion action, the first thing they will ask themselves is, "What's in it for me?" So, if you're able to prove to the consumer buying something gives them an advantage, they will most likely buy it.

    Examples:

    - Show them how much they will save if they buy a product. *Amazon* shows the percentage as well as savings when buying a product.

    - Show them reviews and ratings by verified buyers. If your product has good reviews, the benefits of the product will be reinforced for the visitor.

        Amazon shows reviews and ratings. Users can also filter the reviews from newest to oldest. This way, if there are a lot of reviews, users can opt to see only the newest ones to get an idea about what recent buyers think of the product.

    - Show them comparisons. If there are a lot of websites that sell products like yours, potential customers are going to compare prices, reviews, ratings, etc. before hitting the *Buy* button. Why not make it easier for them by showing them the comparisons right on your website? This can be done by using data from a reliable, well-known comparison website and highlighting the positives related to your website.

6. **The Principle of Authority**
   When someone speaks with authority, people listen. Of course, knowledgeable people will not listen to those who stand on a soapbox and speak loudly. But, if the authority or expertise of the speaker is unquestionable, they will listen, trust and believe.

   In marketing, if your brand is endorsed by someone well-known and very connected with what you are trying to sell, people will believe in your brand.

   Potential customers trust experts who can demonstrate their authority in an area. Wherever possible, display proof of your expertise through trust symbols, FAQs, blogs, etc. When tests show the content of your webpages focusing on educating visitors is getting a lot of attention and people are navigating to your other pages as a result, you will know the content is working.

7. **The Principle of Scarcity**
   Children are naturally attracted to that tin filled with cookies sitting in the kitchen. But the moment they realize there are only one or two cookies left, the appeal of those cookies increases significantly. A similar behavior is also seen in adults. When there is a fear of a potential scarcity, people will rush to stock up.

   In Digital Marketing, when your website visitors are presented with something, they believe will not be available for long, they are more likely to act quickly. The sense of urgency created on the website often prompts the users to go ahead with the conversion.

   Kahneman's Loss Aversion theory also backs up this principle. According to this theory, the fear of losing something drives people to act more than the hope of gaining something.

Examples of using the principle of scarcity to encourage people to act are:

- An offer the user believes is valid only for a short time.

- A user has added a product to the cart but hasn't gone through with the purchase. If the user is told the product is selling fast and might not be available for long, they are likely to act fast.

- An introductory offer that is valid only during their first visit to the website.

- The promise of a gift with purchase, but only if the purchase is made right away.

- A perceived shortage of a certain product, leading the customer to believe they need to stock up.

- A live counter by the product description showing the number of products left.

8. **The Principle of Exclusivity**
   When people feel something is exclusive to them, or to a group or community they belong to, it creates a perception of privilege for them. This is the reason why many people spend thousands of dollars on elite club memberships.

   If you succeed in portraying that something is available for them to buy, is not accessible to many others, this could make them feel compelled to buy it because of the exclusivity attached to it.

9. **The Principle of Impulse**
   What are humans if not impulsive? No matter how careful you are, at one time or another, each one of you has done something on an impulse. You just need a stimulus to trigger your impulsiveness. People are known to buy items impulsively if they are led in the right direction. If your persuasion helps provide stimulus to

the impulsive nature of a person, your conversion is in the bag! Examples of what could trigger impulse shopping are:

- A special sale for the holiday season featuring *unbelievable discounts*.

- An advertisement claiming the website is discounting certain products for the *first time* ever.

- The website is discounting a certain category of products for the *last time*.

- Offering a clearance sale on the website

10. **The Principle of Likability**
It is natural for people to be drawn to something they like and when they like something, it makes the situation conducive for persuasion.

So, they are on your website, and they really like what they see. Now, if you subtly suggest a conversion action, they will mostly likely take it.

But, how do you make your website likable? Well, there are several ways:

- Make the content on your website informal and helpful. It should be something that allows visitors to connect with the brand instead of just having some long-winded text.

- Use pictures your target group can identify with. Before choosing pictures to post on your website, take the demographic of your target group into consideration.

- Work on the overall look of the website. It should be appealing to the audience you are targeting.

Persuasion Considerations

Women as a Target Audience

The principles given earlier cover almost all aspects of persuasion, but what happens when your target group is mostly women? I think you will all agree that men and women are wired differently, and this difference is more apparent in certain situations.

A good example would be of a website that sells clothing. The description for a white casual shirt for men might say *Casual shirt – white*, followed by the fabric type. This is enough of a description for men.

Now, let's look at a white shirt for women. The description would read something like this: "This elegant white shirt has an embroidered collar. It has a concealed, full button placket and a straight hem. Both comfortable and stylish, this shirt can be paired with dark denims and sneakers when you go out with friends, or pair it with a skirt and pumps for an informal dinner. An understated style statement to keep you looking chic."

You can get as creative as you want. Just looking at an image of the shirt wouldn't have the same effect on women as when they *read* about it too.

The Need for Personal Persuasion

Personal Persuasion is all about opening a dialogue between the customers and a representative from the business who can answer any questions they might have. Sometimes, especially during high-value deals, visitors might feel confused and not ready to make the commitment to purchase. At this point, they need personal persuasion. In these cases, encourage visitors to contact your experts either by a chat box or by telephone. If the visitor has previously shared their contact information and given permission to call them, you can have a representative call them to clear up any questions so they will go ahead with the purchase. The whole idea behind this is to have the visitor state the reason behind their hesitation. Even just opening the line for a two-way communication can go a long way in alleviating any doubts and in persuading them to go through with the purchase.

The Role of Content in Persuasion

When used wisely, content is a powerful tool when it comes to persuasion. For exclusive blog sites, content is a make or break aspect of your website. But how you present your business through content in the *About Us* section, FAQ section, and your product descriptions, speaks volumes about your website no matter what type of business it is. Your content needs to inspire the readers. Carefully written content aims at motivating readers to act. It also educates and helps them to decide to take that conversion action.

Reader Engagement

The content must be engaging. Use the element of surprise to ignite the curiosity of the reader so they are motivated enough to keep on reading. The opening paragraph is the most important in this respect so, go all out in writing an appealing opening paragraph. Similarly, the closing paragraph should summarize the important points of your content and should give some sort of conclusion to the entire article. The conclusion should be what convinces the reader to act.

Write simple, easy to read content. Do not use difficult words hoping to sound intellectual and authoritative. This only makes the content more challenging to read and people will usually ignore it. There are many tools available for checking the readability of any content. For example, the *Flesch Reading Ease Formula* rates the content on several factors such as length of the sentences, paragraph structure, active or passive voice used, etc. It is a good idea to aim for content that can easily be processed by students who are between 13 and 15 years of age.

Headline and Sub-headings

The headline of the content should be interesting enough for the reader to want to read further but, it also needs to be specific rather than generic. If you must choose between a clever headline and a practical headline that seeks to meet a customer's need, go for the latter and present some benefit for the reader in the headline. When the reader can easily see reading the content might help them in some way, they will be more interested in spending precious online time in reading all the way through what you have to say.

When you have extremely long content, cut it short. However, if it's necessary that lengthy content is the only way to get your point across, at least divide the content into small, relevant parts by using proper sub-headings. Ideally, each sub-heading should describe a specific benefit for the customer.

Structure your Content

Present information in an easy to scan format. Most readers, even if you call them readers, are not really inclined towards reading the entire content. They normally just skim through it, so you need to structure your content, so it caters to this. Use bullet points and numbered lists to make sure your readers don't miss crucial information.

Intelligently structured content can guide the visitor's movement on your website. For example, you can start with a short, informative article to educate the visitor about the range of your products and credibility. After that, move them on to the information that is more relevant to them then finally narrow things down to their specific needs. You can build a connection with them and answer any questions they may have about your products. During this content-controlled journey, there is a lot of potential to persuade the visitor to hit the buy button at the end.

Persuasion for Repeat Customers or Lifetime Valued Customers

When you speak of customers who have already bought a product or service from a website, let's not jump to the conclusion there is no further need for persuasion. Understand these are the people who were at least once, convinced to spend their money on your website. This, however, does not necessarily mean they will spend money on your website again; you still need to persuade them to do so. Loyal customers are an asset to any business. They not only come to you time after time, but also refer your business to others. Therefore, it would be unwise to think the customers hold no value for the business once the purchase is completed. You can persuade the customer to make a repeat purchase by (a) giving them a good website experience during their initial purchase and (b) following up with them post-sale up to the point when they have used the product or service and have given feedback.

Conclusion

Persuasion must be effortlessly included during all stages of a website visit. So, when a visitor comes to a website, from the trust symbols on the main page, to the little details, up to the point of purchase and beyond, you need to keep proving to them your website is the best option to meet their needs. As a Digital Marketer, you need to look for opportunities to persuade the customers, so they reach this conclusion. Depending on how you use persuasion, there is a potential to establish a true connection with your website visitors. This connection can be established by assuring them you are in tune with their self-interest. Also, let them feel in control during the decision-making phase and through the actual purchase.

When done right, persuasion can help you win eager, loyal customers who *choose* to buy from you every single time.

MOBILE

A decade ago, even though mobile phones could be used for browsing, most users had not warmed up to the idea. Blame it on the smaller screens and poor navigation but, browsing on a mobile was not something people particularly wanted to do because a desktop computer was the more obvious choice. Then, along came tablets and smartphones and the tables turned. With bigger screens that would come to life with a single touch, mobile devices revolutionized the way people used the Internet and phones became much more than devices only good for making and answering calls. With increased features, user friendly interface, and the convenience of carrying it everywhere has ensured smartphones are here to stay.

Understanding Mobile Usage

Desktops and laptops remain relevant for people, but smartphones have become the primary device for most. The number of people using their smartphones for browsing is only increasing, and due to the sheer number of mobile devices, Digital Marketers cannot ignore this growing group of people who now prefer mobile to a desktop or laptop.

People don't just carry their smartphones with them everywhere, they are checking them often, and feel lost without them. For many, it is the last thing they check before going to sleep, and the first thing they look at when they wake up in the morning. They basically have an intimate relationship with their smartphones.

When you talk about building a lasting relationship with the customers through Digital Marketing, you should not forget about the relationship people share with their mobile devices. Acknowledging increased mobile usage is critical from a Digital Marketing perspective. If you don't, you are losing out on an opportunity to connect with these users on a very personal level and, you are losing out on a lot of business.

User intent could be very different when using a desktop than when using a mobile. It depends upon the demographic and circumstances of the visitor. According to the *Pew Internet Research Center*, younger people are more comfortable using their mobiles for all their online activity, while older people still prefer a desktop.

Let's look at some situations where people would use their smartphones or tablets for browsing and how each situation presents different opportunities from a marketing point of view.

1. **Using mobile to kill time**
   People carry their smartphones with them everywhere. Browsing the Internet to kill time is more common than you would think. People turn to their smartphones when bored, nervous, fidgety, or even if they just have some spare time. For example, people use their smartphones to search the Internet while they are in a doctor's waiting room, or in a taxi, or to calm their nerves while waiting for a job interview.

   They might not be browsing out of a specific need, but rather out of boredom. This means they often lack a strong motivation to take any sort of action while browsing.

2. **Using smartphones and tablets as the primary devices for browsing**

   People across all age groups might prefer to use a smartphone or tablet as a primary device, however, it is more common among the younger generation. This group is the one who is most comfortable with using mobile devices for most of their Internet browsing.

   The users who fall in this category are consciously choosing to use their mobile devices for not just casual browsing, but also for specific needs. They often visit websites with the intention of acting. This means the motivation for conversion is already present and they prefer making the conversion action from their mobile devices only.

3. **Using mobiles as a secondary device**

   Some people find it easier and more convenient to make a conversion action from their desktop or laptop, especially if it's one involving money. This is mostly out of habit ingrained from times when online shopping was first introduced and not proven to be trustworthy. However, due to the convenience factor, people might use their smartphones for casual browsing, or even motivated browsing, but would switch to their laptops or desktops when making a purchase. For example, before purchasing a lawn mower, a user might look at different options and compare prices from a mobile device. Then, after zeroing in on the model they want to buy, they might switch over to a desktop or laptop to carry out the purchase.

   In this case, the users are in research mode and are looking for good quality content.

4. **Only using mobile devices when their need is urgent**

   This category of users would generally prefer their desktops or laptops over mobiles, but due to a unique situation, are forced to use their mobile devices. Consider these situations:

   - They are in a new city and want to look for coffee shops in their vicinity.

- They are in a store looking at a new product and want to check the reviews of the product online before buying.

- Their car broke down during a road trip and they want to check where the nearest service station is.

- Their primary browsing device – desktop or laptop – isn't working and they want to contact the customer service center through the website.

In these cases, the user might not be very comfortable with using the mobile device for a solution to their problems, however, they come with the motivation to go through the process. The user intent is usually limited to accessing information of some kind.

The Gap

Digital Marketing primarily revolves around websites, and websites have traditionally been designed for viewing on the larger screens of desktops and laptops. So, when these websites are opened on mobile screens, they neither look good, nor are they user-friendly. The images are too small, the content loads too slowly, or users must scroll left and right to read the text. In short, it's a bad website experience for the users. This creates a gap between what the users need and what mobile websites give them.

For users who rely on smartphones as their primary browsing device, a website not optimized for mobile is an instant turn-off. These websites might not just *look bad*, they could have poor navigation or links that don't work on mobile. In such cases, users might not have the patience to endure the inconvenience and might choose to visit another, more user-friendly site. You may be able to get away with a badly designed mobile site only when a user is accessing it during an emergency, but maybe not even then. After all, almost everybody is optimizing their websites for mobile devices.

TRUE CONNECTIONS

What Does the Increasing Number of Mobile Users Mean for Marketers?

Conversion rates are different for desktops than for mobile devices. This is mainly due to differences in user intent. Even today, the larger number of conversions are still on desktops. Of the total number of conversions for a website, 50% take place on a desktop, 33% are on tablets, and 17% are on smartphones. So, if a website has conversions of 100 per month on a desktop, conversions on a tablet would be around 66, and those on a smartphone would be around 33. That means about 50% of the conversions are from mobile devices. These are approximate numbers based on the total number of mobile users.

The mobile experience is constantly being improved upon. With mobile websites offering the convenience of *one-click-ordering*, and mobile wallets making check-outs faster and easier, mobile conversions are slowly, but steadily, catching up with the desktop in conversions.

The marketers of today cannot have a one-dimensional approach and concentrate only on desktop users. What you need is a Hybrid Approach in the marketing strategy where the audiences on different devices are given customized and effective website experiences. You need to optimize the website for mobile, so you do not lose out on conversions from mobile devices. It takes extra effort, but ultimately, you are ensuring your visitors have a good website experience. Here are some advantages of making the effort to create websites for mobiles:

- **Social media marketing becomes easier**
  Most people have their social media accounts active on their smartphones. This facilitates easy navigation from social media to a web browser and vice versa.

  This means:

  a) With one click, people can visit a website advertised on their social media page. This translates into good traffic for the website.

b) Since social media accounts can be easily integrated, the website experience can be customized for users, which adds more value to their browsing.

c) Due to active social media accounts on smartphones, liking or sharing a webpage becomes easier for users.

- **Users can access information on the go**
  Smartphones are an important part of life for most people. Mobiles make information available to users with a few taps of the screen. They can search, browse, compare, buy, and do almost everything else on a small, handheld device they can do on a desktop. It's convenient and quick.

- **Marketers can reach users quickly**
  Almost every person with a smartphone is in the habit of checking their phones at frequent intervals throughout the day. With such determined regularity in going through the notifications, it is highly unlikely a promotional email will go unnoticed.

- **Mobile websites also help you in Google rankings**
  If you do not have a mobile optimized website, it affects your rankings. Obviously, this impacts your website's visibility in Google searches. This gives you even more of a reason to develop mobile friendly websites!

What Does it Mean to Optimize a Website for Mobile?

Mobile devices have smaller screens and they also respond to touch. Below are a few points that need to be considered in order to develop mobile websites:

1. **Shorten your content**
   When using text to make a point, try to edit the content to a shorter version for mobiles. You already know most users usually scan your text, and this holds true even more for mobile since it only takes

a flick of the thumb to scroll up and down. Also, remember text that looks slightly long on a desktop looks excruciatingly long on the smaller screen of a mobile.

2. **Break the content into smaller chunks with images for support**
   In order to adapt to the users' tendency to just scan through content, break it up into easy-to-read sections with concise sub-headings letting the user know what each section covers. Also, mobile users rely on visual cues. Use relevant images for each section so the user knows what to expect so the visitor can quickly get to the information they need.

3. **Be aware of the layout**
   You need to pay careful attention to the site's layout. Things that appear fine on a larger desktop screen might appear disjointed or crowded on a mobile screen. Pay close attention to how the text and images are situated on the mobile site. Also, make sure the CTA button is clearly visible above the bottom of the home screen.

4. **Use appropriate images**
   Using images on mobile sites has its advantages, but pictures that take too long to load must be avoided. Make sure images load quickly and keep in mind images that look good on a desktop website might be too small for a mobile site. Of course, users can zoom on an image to take a closer look but, that takes away some of the convenience. Only use pictures that will be easy to see on mobile screens.

   Sometimes websites use text superimposed on images. This works on a large monitor, but when the same website is viewed on a mobile, the text may not be clearly visible. To avoid this, separate the text and the image for mobile sites.

5. **For telephone numbers**
   We have already discussed the importance of placing the telephone number at the top of your webpage as a trust symbol. When placing the phone number on mobile sites, don't forget smartphones can

make a call. So, when users click on the telephone number from their smartphones, it would be ideal if the number is a link to allow the call to automatically to go through. In this way, they don't have to write it down.

This is a small detail, but it plays a part in making things much easier for users, which helps to give them a good website experience.

6. **Use videos**
   The tech savvy, smartphone carrying users are more open to watching videos giving them a better understanding of what you're saying so, videos work well in mobile marketing. However, let the visitors decide if they want to play the video or not. Don't just have it start automatically and without warning.

7. **Mobile searches**
   Be aware desktop and mobile searches are two different things. Since mobile devices have an option to activate location services, when a user searches for something from a mobile device, they should also get location-specific results.

8. **Be mindful of the size of the buttons**
   Remember users are going to use their fingers, and often their thumbs, to click on the buttons on a mobile device. If you make the buttons so small that users need to zoom in on the screen to tap the button, then you need to make sure those users have an extremely strong motivation to make the effort. Or, you can simply make the buttons larger!

9. **Make sure mobile websites load quickly**
   Today, people have the patience and attention span of a toddler. If you don't give them what they need quickly, they will lose interest. Make sure the mobile sites do not take forever to load!

Mobile Apps vs Mobile Websites

For every business that has a website, one of the factors to keep in mind while developing a site for mobile devices is whether to develop an app, or a just a responsive mobile site. Unfortunately, there is no right answer to this.

Mobile websites are simply extensions of desktop versions. They have a responsive design to make them adaptable to any mobile device and run on whichever browser the mobile device supports.

Apps, on the other hand, need to be developed separately and users need to download them from the *Google Playstore*, *iOS App Store*, etc., depending on the device's operating system.

Many people believe an app is the answer to all their mobile requirements and the App is perceived as the ultimate solution to conversion woes. The reality is there is no *perfect* solution. You need to evaluate what works best for the business.

There are a few points you need to consider while deciding on what would work for you. Don't write off mobile websites completely just because Apps sound more convenient and modern. A few advantages to developing a mobile website over an app are:

1. **Mobile websites do not need separate customization for different operating systems.**
   You don't need to develop different versions for Androids, iPhones, Blackberry phones. A well-developed mobile site is compatible across all platforms.

2. **Mobile websites are found in search results.**
   The app you develop for your website will not come up when a user performs a search. A mobile website has a better chance of being found by search engines. So, if you're not *Amazon*, or *Netflix*, or anyone else who doesn't need an introduction, a mobile website is a must so people can find you in search results.

3. **Mobile websites are instantly available.**
   Unlike an app, users don't need to download and install a website. They can simply open it in the browser, so there is zero wait time once they decide to click on the website's link.

4. **Updates and upgrades are automatic.**
   Users don't have to worry about updating a mobile website. The moment they open the site, they have the updated version right in front of them.

5. **Mobile websites have better reach.**
   All users might not have an app, but all of them have a browser on their mobile device. The mobile website has the potential to reach everyone in the target group without them having to go through a separate download.

6. **Mobile websites cannot be deleted when you close it**
   The user may close the browser window once they are done viewing the website, but it will still be there if they decide to view it again. All they need to do is just open it again in the browser.

7. **Mobile websites are less expensive compared to apps.**
   If you have major budget constraints, app development and support could prove to be way too expensive, forcing you to drop the idea and go with a mobile website only.

Scenarios in Which Mobile Websites Are the Way to Go

It's not always just about the advantages of mobile websites that were discussed above. Sometimes, it's also about whether you really should have a mobile app.

For instance, if you have a website where the primary goal is creating brand awareness through content, a mobile website might work just fine. Other examples where a mobile website would work are:

- Websites where the CTA is a subscription for a non-digital magazine or newspaper.

- Websites where users register for newsletters to be delivered via email.

- Websites featuring useful content, but not something people would need or want regularly, such as instructions for DIY projects.

- Websites giving information about educational institutions like colleges or universities.

Mobile Apps

Sometimes, an app is the way to go for boosting conversions and reaching your marketing goals. Apps must be downloaded from the app store on a smartphone or tablet but, if users are given enough incentive, needing to download the app would not be a deterrent. Generally, users wouldn't give too much thought to downloading an app, however, once the app is installed, it doesn't take much to annoy those users into deleting it!

Apps have some definite advantages over mobile websites. Users find them convenient to use, they are faster and more efficient, and they can be customized according to the users' preferences. Let's look at some of the advantages of having a mobile app:

1. **Customization**
   When a user downloads an app, they can be given plenty of options to choose from in order to customize their experience. Users can personalize the app as to its appearance complete with accurate details. Each person can even customize the content to show only what is relevant to them. Customization enhances the app's usability and as a marketer, you can carry out a very specific, customized marketing strategy for each user.

2. **Notifications**

   When an app is downloaded, it can send out two types of notifications:

   - Push Notifications – These are the notifications the app sends to the home screen, even when the app is not in use. They are great for: reminders (*Sale ends in 3 hours!*), promotional messages (*Here's a discount coupon for the weekend sale!*), news about a specific event (*Coming to your city for a special event this weekend*), personalized messages (*Here are some products found especially for you*). When downloading the app, users must allow Push Notifications. If they do allow these notifications, users can turn them off at any time. The good news is statistically, many users allow Push Notifications when they install the app, so marketers need to take care not to overuse the notifications. If their smartphone beeps every few hours with a notification which the user finds irrelevant, the user will certainly turn off the notification. Worse, they will delete the app altogether. So, make the notifications count, but don't overdo it.

   - In-App Notifications - In-App Notifications are the messages users get when they open the app or when they are using the app. They are useful when you want the users to get involved with your brand through certain content pieces. These notifications can also come in handy when you want the users to know about any new features added to the app and remind them of the update available.

3. **Regular use**

   If your business is one where users need to come to repeatedly, an app works well. The app is a separate entity existing on a user's mobile device. This eliminates competition to some extent. For example, if a user trusts a brand enough to download their app, chances are they would use the app every time they want to make a purchase and not bother with the search-browse-compare-buy cycle. Think about a grocery shopping website. If someone is buying their weekly or monthly groceries from the Amazon Pantry via the Amazon app, they probably won't be interested in using another website or app whenever it's time to place their order.

4. **Interactive use**

   In cases where a lot of interaction between a user and the website is required, an app makes more sense. Think dating, gaming and social media websites. It is much more convenient for a user to have an app on their mobile device where they can save their preferences, their gaming scores, their social media saves, etc.

5. **Offline access to some content**

   An app can make certain content available to users even when they are offline. Information about their past orders, or specific content that was saved for later viewing can be accessed by users when they do not have an internet connection. For example, online music websites let you listen to saved music from their apps even when offline.

6. **No need to log-in every time**

   Once a user installs an app and registers on it, there is no need to enter the login credentials each time they want to access it. Apps with sensitive data such as banking apps, or even email apps, can be made more secure by enabling enhanced security features.

7. **In-app purchases**

   In order to boost sales, users can be offered in-app purchases. An example of this would be a gaming app where users are given the option to buy more *lives* in order to advance in a game. Or, users could opt to pay for certain features not available in the free version of the app.

Where Would an App Work Best?

1. **Banking apps**
   Banking apps provide a great deal of convenience for users by bringing almost all banking services to the tip of their fingers. Apps, compared to banking websites, provide better accessibility and are easier to use. They also provide better security and the feature allowing alerts on transactions can be very helpful.

2. **E-commerce apps**
   When you have an app for e-commerce, it becomes easier for the user to customize the buying experience. E-commerce apps from retail giants such as Amazon, Walmart, eBay, and Target are very popular today. What's more, research results done by *Criteo* shows e-commerce app conversion rates are three times higher than those from mobile websites (Criteo, Americas, Q1 2018 Review).

3. **Media (music or video) apps**
   It is extremely convenient to have an app for websites providing audio/visual content. Look at how popular the YouTube app is! YouTube, as a video sharing website, already had a huge fan base when the app was launched. Now, however, almost everybody with a mobile device prefers the YouTube app because it's so convenient to use!

4. **Gaming**
   For games, an app makes much more sense than a website. The gaming experience can be greatly improved via an app. The proof of this lies in the rise of gaming apps available over the last few years, and the fact people download these apps in staggering numbers.

5. **News**
   In an era when people don't have time to go through entire newspapers every day, it helps to have news apps on smartphones where users can have their news on the go in compressed formats, or choose whether they want to read the business, sports, or political sections. Also, due to customized notifications, users can

have that important piece of information instantly. Even though newspaper websites are quite popular, news apps win!

6. **Social media**

    Social media websites are hugely popular across all age groups, and with the introduction of apps, connecting with people has never been easier. In times when people want speed in browsing, posting, liking or sharing something on social media, apps are an obvious choice.

7. **Dating**

    Dating websites need to be interactive and customizable. Because of this, an app is preferred. It is much easier to upload pictures, chat with people and define your preferences. Users can also choose to set up alerts, which is an added advantage.

Problems with Apps

Apps are great, but they do come with their own set of problems. When users download an app, they expect a lot from it. They expect it to be faster than the mobile website so, when users come across apps taking too long to load, they will probably delete it if the problem persists more than a couple of times.

Similarly, if the app takes up too much memory and impacts the function of the smartphone, tablet and any other apps, users will surely give up on the problem app. The same applies to apps that keep crashing.

Users also expect the app to give them some value over the mobile website. So, if the app doesn't have essential features, users will be unhappy, to say the least.

The Mobile App marketplace shows ratings and reviews for every app. In cases of similar apps vying for users' attention, the one with better ratings and reviews obviously gets downloaded more. From a marketing perspective, it's important to be aware of user feedback about the app. The app also needs to be upgraded on a regular basis to remove bugs and make it more user-friendly.

How good or bad an app is, says a lot about the business. People are almost always willing to download an app, with the idea it will make things easier for them, which is a throwback to Chapter 1 where there was discussion how all people are selfish. Most people downloading the app that you developed, do so for their own self-interest. They don't download it so you can convince them to buy something; they download so they get what they came for, and then some. So, make sure the app is designed by keeping the user in mind.

App development is expensive and so is its maintenance and support. So, think carefully about the budget you can set aside for the maintenance because, NO app is better than a bad app.

Emails on Smartphones

With more people depending on smartphones as their primary device for sending and receiving emails, sending emails that work for mobile becomes mandatory for you. You need to optimize your emails anticipating they will be viewed on a mobile device.

The first thing to take into consideration is the email notifications feature on mobile. Usually, users are notified as soon as there is something new in their inboxes. A notification appears on the home screen containing the sender's name, the subject line, and a small snippet of the body for the email. What you want is to have a subject line that is relevant and interests the user. Also, the snippet should either intrigue the recipient or provide some value.

Also, remember the CTA should be above the fold even in emails. If the users don't quickly see the point you are trying to make in the email, they are sure to ignore it and most likely forget about it.

Make email content easier to see on a mobile device. Make sure the font and CTA buttons aren't too small for viewing on a mobile screen. Care should be taken that the formatting is aesthetic enough to be viewed on a mobile. In the event the mobile device does not support the format in which the email is created, give the user an option to open the content in a browser where it can be viewed better.

It's also very important to make sure you let the recipients control the frequency of your emails.

Protect the Users' Data

Mobile marketing, whether through mobile websites or apps, provide the company an opportunity to collect user data. However, you must understand the privacy concerns of your customers. Use the data you have collected only with their permission. After all, you are trying to build a relationship with your customer, and they deserve and expect this kind of sensitivity from you. Consider the below points:

- Understand the type of data being collected.

- Establish who the owner of the data is. If your technology service provider allows you to be the data owner, you are in a better position to protect user data.

- Establish how you can use the data to segment your customers.

Make sure you do not have any data gaps during the execution of your approach. Never forget users attach a lot of importance to privacy, so don't give them any cause to mistrust you.

Final Advice

Mobile devices have made life much easier for people, but it also has made them look for instant gratification. The result of this is the patience levels and attention spans are at an all-time low. People simply do not have the time to go through everything that appears on their smartphones or tablets. This poses a challenge to marketing. What's the use of developing clever strategies if the users are just going to ignore or delete something you show them with a single swipe? To overcome this, always remember that whatever you expose users to, should be created with *their* needs as the focus. Understand there are no prizes for a clever marketing strategy if there are no conversions among your customers or target group. Making everything interesting and easy to process, is the basis of getting people to use their mobile devices to convert which you are so keen on!

USING TECHNOLOGY

If you can't measure something, you can't hope to manage or improve upon it. Therefore, in Digital Marketing, there are two things you need to measure: website performance and user experience. Conversion Rate Optimization (CRO) is a continuous process and it leans heavily on the monitoring of different metrics. The success of your CRO strategy can be measured by keeping track of these different metrics.

The first step to a good CRO program is to clearly define the key metrics or key performance indicators (KPIs) based on the program goals. By using KPIs, you can track and measure the results of your efforts and learn if you are getting closer to achieving your CRO goals and measure the value of your activities for the business.

In CRO, the KPIs can be divided into two categories:

- Macro Conversions, or the primary goals of the website, and
- Micro Conversions, or the secondary goals

Macro conversions are the ultimate actions you want visitors to take on your website. These can vary depending on the nature of your business. If you have an eCommerce site, for instance, the macro conversion is the purchase or sale. If you are in B2B, then it could be the request for a quote or lead contact submission.

Micro conversions are the actions visitors take before getting to the final conversion action. These are the steps leading visitors deeper into the funnel, such as clicking on your email, downloading a free whitepaper, subscribing to the blog, or even following the business page on social channels.

In this section, how you can use different technology and tools to track and measure how your website and online marketing campaigns are faring against your KPIs will be presented. In turn, your key performance indicators will show you how close you are getting towards your goals or where you need to focus your optimization efforts to get there.

Within Google Analytics, for instance, you can monitor key website metrics by device type and source:

- **Bounce Rate** – the percentage of visitors leaving the website after viewing only one page.

- **Exit Rate** – the percentage of visitors leaving the website after navigating through more than one page on the site.

- **Time Spent on the Site** – the total duration of time a visitor spends on a website. It gives a clear indication of the level of interest the website generates for the visitor.

- **Pages Per Session** – the average number of pages a visitor goes through on a website during one session. A lower number indicates low engagement and interest in the website, whereas a higher number would mean the visitor is interested enough to explore the website.

- **Goals** – SMART (Specific, Measurable, Achievable, Relevant, Time-bound) goals need to be decided upon by the marketer/

business owner, which can be actively monitored during the marketing campaign.

- **E-Commerce** – the commercial transactions taking place on a website.

You will learn about the popular tools used by data-driven marketers and businesses to continually improve their website and online experience.

Web Analytics

Web analytics is the process of collecting, organizing, and reporting data on user behavior. It helps in increasing the number of visitors and/or customers, customer retention, and improved CRO. It is an effective market research tool that can be used to plan the marketing strategy aligned with the business goals. It also helps measure changes in the website performance after a new marketing campaign and enables you to estimate these changes prior to the campaign launch.

Some of the popular Web Analytics services are:

- **Google Analytics** – It is a Google service providing analytical data and tools that can help towards Search Engine Optimization (SEO) and better digital marketing strategies.

- **Adobe Analytics** – This service from Adobe provides useful insights based on data related to visitor activity on the website.

- **IBM Digital Analytics (Formerly IBM Coremetrics)** – This is an IBM service providing analytics data related to multi-channel marketing as well as visitor's activities on a website.

- **Chart Mogul** – It is an analytics service that specifically deals with subscriptions on a website.

- **Mixpanel** – It is a tool providing tracking data on visitors' behavior on a desktop or mobile website.

- **VWO (Visual Website Optimizer)** – It provides a platform to create a CRO strategy based on user data and continuously monitor and test improvements.

What Should You Look for in the Web Analytics Reports?

The data collected from Web Analytics will only be useful if you know what to look for that matters to your business. If you have an e-commerce site, for instance, you will obviously want to track your conversions from actual sales as opposed to blog page views. Below are some of the other things you can track in your analytics dashboard in order to get meaningful insights on user behavior and your site performance:

1. **Visitor actions on mobile**
   Your web analytics tool should be able to tell you whether your visitors use multiple devices to visit your site and if they do, which types of mobile devices most of them are using. From here, you will want to see what they are doing when they are on your site:

   - Are they searching for something specific? This is usually the case if they use your search bar a lot

   - Do you get a lot of browsing of your product detail pages but few conversions? This could indicate your visitors are comparison-shopping, which means you might need to create a mobile-compare function to make your visitors' lives easier

   - Do they add to cart but never complete checkout? This is usually the case when they're using the cart to store items, they're interested in buying, maybe not right now but later. You might need to make sure your visitors' carts don't expire too soon or prompt them to create an account so they can save the cart contents for later

These are just some examples of the mobile-specific behaviors you want to track within analytics so you can improve the experience for mobile device users.

2. **Know where your visitors are bouncing**
   If you are already tracking your bounce rate, you will also want to see exactly *where* your visitors are bouncing off your site. You can track this by monitoring the exit pages on Google Analytics, but most other tools should also have this capability. By learning which pages your visitors are bouncing on, you can determine if the pages need to be improved in terms of content, usability, or overall relevance for your target audience. In Google Analytics, you can visualize the visitor's journey on your site by looking at the behavior flow.

   Knowing the drop-off points is crucial to resolving common experience issues encountered by visitors on your site. If you have a shopping cart on your site, for instance, you'll want to see which parts of the cart have the highest exit rates - which translates to leaks in your conversion funnel. Once you have this information, you can then fix the problems and stop losing potential customers just as they are about to convert.

3. **Know which terms are searched for the most**
   Knowing the terms that people type into the search box is one of your best sources of learning what they're interested in. Considering up to 20% of your visitors will use the search function on your site, it's important you enable site search tracking in your analytics tool. Some ways you can use the on-site search data to improve your site are:

   - Discover the most popular items or products based on the **terms people enter the most**. Once you have this data, you can run a test featuring these products. In this way, visitors won't have to waste time searching for them. Or, you can improve your navigation so visitors can find these items easily.

   - Learn which terms people type in and then **leave without clicking on any of the results**. This indicates they were not satisfied with the search results. You can then improve the results for the terms searched, or, you can create featured results using those terms in order to improve the website experience.

4. **High traffic and bounce areas**
   If you are generating a lot of traffic on some of your pages, you need to check them for bounce rates. This way, you will know if some of these pages are broken and need to be fixed. Otherwise, you might be losing out on a lot of potential conversions because of problems with user experience on these high-traffic areas.

   Fixing or improving these broken, high-traffic pages is one of the easiest things to do when it comes to conversion rate optimization. Doing this is time and energy well-spent as it brings a ton of value to your site.

5. **The error recovery rate**
   What happens when a user encounters the *404 – Page not found* error on your website? Do they immediately exit the website after the error page, or are they willing to stay on and explore other parts of the website? You must measure the exit rate on the error pages to get the answer. A high exit rate is a clear indication of your failure to help the visitor recover from the error page.

   What you need is an error page that is helpful. From time to time, a user might get a 404 Error. When that happens, don't depend on the programmer-designed error message to notify them. Provide a human touch by briefly explaining to them what has happened, and then give them enough prompts to get them connected again.

   Just by trying to be friendly with visitors when they encounter an error page, you will be surprised to see a severe drop in the exit rate. On the other hand, an error message has a sense of finality to it making visitors feel they have reached a dead end and they will likely close the website.

6. **The search depth**
   How many search levels do visitors go to in order to find what they need? This is an important metric because it shows whether the search filters you have in place are helping visitors narrow down their searches towards increasingly relevant products. A further careful analysis of this metric, coupled with the bounce rate, will enable patterns to emerge so you know which searches are contributing to a bad user experience on the website.

Usability Tests

Usability tests help identify the pitfalls from a user perspective when you launch new features or design changes to a website. The sample size is usually small, but the outcome helps to assess the practicality of the changes. The metrics that can be measured through usability tests are:

Task Completion Rate

A participant can be asked to complete a task on the website. Then, you can check what obstacles they faced in completing this task, and in doing so, identify the problems with the website.

Time per Task

You can measure the time taken by a participant to complete different tasks. After the same tasks have been performed by different users, the tasks taking the most time can be identified. Further analysis can reveal why the users take more time to figure out the task, and how the website can be improved to make things easier.

How to Test Your Website

When designers create a website, they have some expectations in mind. Testing helps you see how the website is performing in relation to what you expected.

Tools Hierarchy

Below is a list of tools in a general hierarchy. The tools given are only for the sake of explanation and can be replaced by a similar tool of the same type.

Stage 1 - Google Search Console

This is the most basic tool you can use. Google Search Console (GSC) can be used even in cases where there isn't enough traffic to create samples for useful testing. It can also be used to optimize site visibility.

GSC has features that help marketers to:

- Identify errors in a sitemap
- Look at the keywords bringing visitors to the website
- Assign country specific URLs
- Make sure the most important pages within the website can be indexed
- Check security issues
- List internal and external pages the site is linked to, etc.

This stage lays the foundation for further tests by giving you enough information to work with.

Stage 2 - Web Analytics Tools

Services such as Google Analytics, Adobe Analytics, etc. can be used for web analytics. During testing, Web analytics tools help you get information about a few things related to your website that can help you In decision-making:

- Which pages get the most traffic?

- What is the source of the traffic?

- Which pages get a lot of user engagement?

- Which pages contribute to the most conversions?

This stage basically tells you what is happening on the site.

Stage 3 – Survey Tools

Surveys provide a means to connect and interact with the user. They help you explore further into the thought process and behavior of the website users. Surveys answer questions such as:

- What are people looking for when they come to the website?

- How many users find what they need?

- What parts of the website prove to be problem areas?

- Which tasks do users find most difficult to complete?

- How good or bad is the website experience for users based on an overall rating of satisfaction?

To get detailed information like this, services such as Google Analytics alone will not suffice. What you need is a VOC (Voice of Customer) tool enabling you to get the answers directly from the users.

Stage 4 – Usability Testing Tools

There are a multitude of usability tests you can run to make sure your website not only works, but also meets user expectations. Contrary to popular belief, you don't need to have a lot of users to get significant insights about your site. In fact, usability expert Jakob Nielsen suggests you can get most of your insights from testing no more than five users and allocating your budget to running as many small tests as possible. You just need to make sure you have the right situations and goals for usability testing to be productive.

Why you shouldn't jump to Stage 4

The timing of the testing is crucial. You need to have adequate past data to be able to base your tests on it. In the above hierarchy of tools, the first three stages provide enough information to make using the testing tools worthwhile.

Additional Tools

There are quite a lot of tools available, but you should carefully choose the most relevant, which would give the best outcome at any given point.

The following methods help you have a deeper understanding of user behavior online:

Heat Mapping

Heat mapping and eye tracking tools enable you to see where a visitor is looking, scrolling, and clicking.

Heat maps indicate high-and-low level activity on a webpage using colors to represent the activity levels. These maps are very useful in understanding which parts of the website attract the most attention while showing what goes unnoticed. It not only helps in measuring the performance, it also helps in designing websites that are user-friendly and practical.

There are several heat mapping tools available for you to choose from:

- Hotjar
- Crazy Egg
- Inspectlet

- Mouseflow

- Lucky Orange

- Clicktale

- VWO

- Feng-GUI

- Zoho

Session Recording

Any Digital Marketer would give their right arm to get inside the minds of visitors to know how they think. While technology hasn't yet made it humanly possible to do that, it has made it possible to literally look over the shoulder of the user when they are on your website. This is done through Session Recording. With the detailed report Session Recording provides, it's easy to see how quickly, if at all, the visitor finds something interesting on the website. It can also answer the critical question for you: *why exactly does a visitor not convert?*

A typical Session Recording report holds details about each user's unique activity on the website including the pages they visited, the total time spent on each page, etc. It can also indicate whether the website was accessed through a mobile device or a desktop. If you want to observe the online activity of the visitor on an even deeper level, you can play the recorded session and see exactly how the visitor browsed the website.

Different Session Recording tools available are:

- Hotjar

- Crazy Egg

- Inspectlet

- Mouseflow
- Lucky Orange
- Clicktale
- VWO

User Panels

User Panels do not only let you see what a visitor does on your website, they also let you hear what visitors think about it. They are usually in the form of workshops encouraging a conversation between the service provider and the users. It is a way to get feedback on the existing model, discuss ideas for improvement, and listen to opinions about projected changes. While it gives a better representation of the end users in the grand scheme of things, it often does not give a true picture of user intent. However, it is very effective in highlighting poor UX design.

Different user panels available are:

- usertesting.com
- UserBob
- USERBRAIN
- VALIDATELY
- userfeel.com
- 99tests.com

Split and Multivariate Testing

Split and multivariate testing comes in after you have determined your website works well and is ready to start converting visitors. At this stage, you can run experiments using control and variation pages on visitor groups to see which ones perform well, and then refine your pages for conversion elements based on the results.

When done the right way, split and multivariate testing helps you determine which combinations work best for conversions.

Split, or A/B Tests

The basic components of an A/B test are a control and a variation page. The control page is usually a high-traffic page that's suffering from either a high bounce rate or a low conversion rate. It's important to choose a page worth fixing so your effort is not wasted. The variation page is like the control page but with a few tweaks, or refinements, based on reliable theories of conversion-oriented website design.

As the name suggests, the traffic is split so half gets sent to the control page while the other half goes to the variation page. The performance of the page is then observed and measured over time, based on a key metric (e.g. bounce rate, click-through or conversion rate). When enough time has elapsed where an adequate sample group has interacted with each page, one of the pages is declared a winner.

Multivariate Tests

Multivariate tests (MVTs) are like split tests, but instead of testing one variable between two pages, MVTs test different combinations of web elements at the same time. Instead of just one variation, you can test multiple variations of a landing page against the control page and split the traffic among them.

One thing to keep in mind with multivariate testing is the traffic requirement. Even with basic split testing, you need at least 10 conversions per day to ensure the statistical validity and reliability of your tests.

If you're just starting out, it might be a better idea to focus on improving the overall usability of your website and worry about split or multivariate testing later, when you have the traffic needed for these kinds of tests.

Different testing tools available are:

- VWO
- Unbounce
- Optimizely
- Maxymiser
- Adobe Test & Target
- SiteSpect
- A/B Tasty
- Google Analytics, Optimize & Adwords
- Zoho

Personalization

Personalization tools help you to have a one-on-one dialogue with visitors and allow you to customize *each visitor's website experience.* This personalized interaction goes a long way in enhancing the overall website experience and boosting conversions.

Personalization is a very important factor if you want to provide an omni-channel digital experience. It lets you present different experiences to your visitors based on the device they're using, location, touchpoint, or data from their previous visits. For instance, you can show different content to people who access your site from a desktop than those using a mobile device. You can also present different content to returning visitors versus first-time visitors to your landing page.

With advances in Artificial Intelligence (AI) technology, you can expect the arrival of highly sophisticated tools that can predict customer needs and behavior, and accordingly, deliver the right content in the right context.

The tools currently available for personalization are:

- Evergage
- Optimizely Personalization
- Google Optimize 360
- Dynamic Yield
- Monetate
- Apptus
- Adobe Target
- Personyze

Exit Pop-ups

Exit pop-ups are windows that are triggered when visitors are about to leave a website and are a common example of onsite retargeting tools. They are a last-ditch attempt to convince the visitor to stay, and possibly convert. Just when the visitor is losing interest and is about to leave the website, an exit pop-up will help you re-engage with them.

The key to an effective exit pop-up is to include an irresistible offer or incentive that would compel the visitor to stay on the website and complete either a micro or macro-conversion action.

Pop-up tools currently available are:

- OptinMonster
- OptiMonk
- Wishpond
- Privy
- Wisepops

Surveys

Surveys can help you gain valuable insights into what a random subset of users think about your website. The best time to launch a survey is at the point when the visitor is exiting your website. If it is launched immediately after the visitor lands on the website, it's much too early for them to be able to answer the survey questions. Besides, this would be annoying. If the survey catches the visitor during active navigation, it will distract them. So, once the visitor has seen everything they want to see (maybe they've even taken a conversion action) and are ready to leave, that is when the survey would get the best possible response.

There are several tools available that you can use to launch surveys. Some are basic tools you can customize to suit your needs and some tools are elaborate ones with stock questions and provisions for videos of user sessions. You can choose whichever one suits your requirements the best. Some of the more popular survey tools are:

- KissMetrics
- SurveyMonkey
- Typeform

- Google forms

- Zoho

Surveys open a window into user experience through the right questions. Too many questions, however, are a surefire way to either get the visitor to quit the survey midway, or worse, get inaccurate responses from them just because they want to finish it quickly. For a successful survey, you need an optimum number of well-worded questions to help get the most accurate information out of your visitors.

The important information that you can observe through surveys include:

Ability to complete the task

1. What is it the visitor was looking for on the website? This could be a list of products, services, or information.

2. Did the user find it? This could be a simple yes or no question.

User satisfaction

1. How easy it was to find what they were looking for? This could be a revelation to you and indicate whether your design is really working in the real world.

2. How was their experience in navigating the website?

Net promoter score

1. How likely is the user to recommend your website to others? Knowing the answer to this would tell you how the website really made the visitor feel.

System Usability Scale

Created by John Brooke in 1986, the System Usability Scale (SUS) measures overall usability utilizing a Likert scale questionnaire with standardized content based on a user satisfaction index. The SUS was designed as a low-cost, "quick and dirty" method for evaluating the usability of virtually any kind of system.

The major benefit of the SUS is it can be administered quickly and cheaply, online, so you can easily gather statistically valid data for scoring your website. Your website visitors will be asked 10 questions, which they need to answer by ranking their level of agreement with each statement on a scale of 1 to 5, with 1 being strong disagreement and 5 being strong agreement. The questions are as follows:

1. I think that I would like to use this system frequently.
2. I found the system unnecessarily complex.
3. I thought the system was easy to use.
4. I think I would need the support of a technical person to be able to use this system.
5. I found the various functions in this system were well integrated.
6. I thought there was too much inconsistency in this system.
7. I would imagine that most people would learn to use this system very quickly.
8. I found the system very cumbersome to use.
9. I felt very confident using the system.
10. I needed to learn a lot of things before I could get going with this system.

TRUE CONNECTIONS

Once you have completed gathering data from website visitors, you can then calculate your website's usability score. The method for this, according to Brooke's original paper is:

"To calculate the SUS score, first sum the score contributions from each item. Each item's score contribution will range from 0 to 4. For items 1,3,5,7, and 9 the score contribution is the scale position minus 1. For items 2,4,6,8 and 10, the contribution is 5 minus the scale position. Multiply the sum of the scores by 2.5 to obtain the overall value of SU."

Simply put:

- Add all scores for each item

- Subtract 1 from the score of each of the odd numbered questions.

- Subtract the value of each of the even numbered questions from 5.

- Take these new values and add up the total score. Then multiply this by 2.5.

After doing this, you have your score, with 100 being the highest. The average System Usability Scale score is 68. If your website scores below this, then you should consider there are serious usability issues on your site.

Diagnosis of Greedy Marketer Syndrome

If you're still not sure whether you have *Greedy Marketer Syndrome*, you can use the technology available for an accurate diagnosis.

Some symptoms that are a dead giveaway are:

1. The educational or informational content is too thin. There's only enough to get some organic traffic to the website, but inadequate to be of any real use for the visitors.

2. The Bounce Rate is quite high. Visitors are leaving the website without doing much.

If you look within Google Search Console, you can see which keywords bring the traffic to your site. Compare these with the content you have in order to know whether you are really delivering on what you promised. You can essentially lower the bounce rate by focusing on all stages in the funnel, instead of being greedy and concentrating only on the bottom.

Marketing Tools

Just having a website isn't enough. You also need to maintain it. Manual website management is time consuming, but there are tools available that can be used for more convenient and automated website management. Even though these tools don't take manual intervention out of the equation completely, they sure save a lot of time for you.

1. **Customer relationship management tools**
   Managing your relationship with your customers is as important as having one. It helps you in serving the customers better. Customer Relationship Management (CRM) tools help you automate some of the tasks you need for effective relationship management. You can achieve the following through a good CRM tool:

   - Tracking communication with the customer for a better organized marketing campaign.

   - Making sure that all salespeople are on the same page, so customers don't receive duplicate contact. All salespeople must know about any previous communications with the customer.

   - Sending marketing material automatically to the customers as per the settings.

TRUE CONNECTIONS

2. **Tools for performance improvement**
   Website performance issues need to be weeded out regularly. There are tools available that can monitor website performance and highlight any problems. These tools can automate the monitoring process. As a result, you become aware of the problems with the website before a lot of visitors are exposed to them. With some luck, you can correct the issues before they affect many visitors.

   For example, AppDynamics from Cisco is one such tool that identifies slow response time on a website. Slow response time drives customers away from websites, with more than 50% of them never returning. It also affects the rankings of the website. So, a tool that accurately and quickly reports on these issues, helps greatly in preventing further damage.

   Another example is Advanced LinkFixer. It helps identify broken links on a website and fixes them. Broken links leave a bad impression on your visitors by making your website appear unprofessional. A tool to quickly get to the broken links and fix them makes for a seamless website experience for visitors.

3. **Tools for updating content**
   Updating content is important for any website, but, more so for content-driven websites. It helps to provide regular visitors with something new every time and it also improves organic traffic. Tools are available helping you automatically update content, create posts from notes on a synced smartphone, create calendar events, or repurpose old content. *If This Then That* (IFTTT) and *Zapier* are tools that can help you with this.

4. **Tools for email marketing**
   Email marketing is an effective method of online marketing, however, manually sending emails to all your leads/subscribers is practically impossible. Automation tools available that send out marketing emails in bulk are a huge help. You can also personalize the emails (address each recipient by their name), as well as segment

the marketing based on various factors. Tools such as *MailChimp* and *Constant Contact* can be used for email marketing automation.

5. **Technical management tools**
   The right tools can also help in automating some infrastructure management. These tools can make the programmers' job a little bit easier by allowing them to automate some parts of the technical aspects of website management.

   For example, tools such as *Pantheon* can be used to keep the website's code updated. It also provides user interfaces for effective management, which helps keep everybody on the team on the same page.

Summary

Technology has made it possible to do quite a few marketing tasks automatically, and many tasks can be done far more quickly using the appropriate tools. With Digital Marketing gaining more and more traction with each passing year, the tools available are also increasing in number and becoming more and more sophisticated and accurate. When you use the correct tools, it gives a much-needed boost to your marketing. It reduces the marketing time and cost by eliminating manual effort to a large extent and it frees up these resources to be constructively used for better results.

STUPID HUMAN TRICKS

Humans are not only selfish; they are also stupid. However, the stupidity is usually hidden. But when it clouds the decision-making ability and it combines with selfishness, the problems begin.

Digital Marketers think they are being clever when they come up with strategies that can only be stupid, but they forget they can no longer get away with fooling customers. Even though people have low attention spans, it hardly means they are gullible. The truth is people are weary of everything they see online, and they are careful about where they spend their money. They are more aware of their choices, and they have plenty of resources to help them make informed decisions. The world is a smaller place because of the internet and Digital Marketers know this. The problem is they don't really understand it. They don't recognize the implications of using tricks to attract customers.

The thing is, there is a percentage of users that sometimes fall for these tricks, and when they do, marketers milk the situation for all it's worth. Sometimes, they even succeed in making a quick buck or two for the business. But what happens in the long run? Something they didn't expect, long term losses.

Stupid tricks might get you a few gullible customers, but by concentrating on this very small percentage of people, you are losing out on the larger target group. That group is probably moving on to your competitor, who is not trying to trick them into anything. If your Digital Marketing strategy relies on stupid tricks, you most likely have dissatisfied customers, who are never coming back to you.

Don't Annoy People

Imagine that you are invited to someone's home for dinner. You graciously accept the invitation and arrive on time. Then, the moment you reach their doorstep, your host switches on some bright, colorful lights as a welcome. You shield your eyes at the sudden brightness, but the host then waves banners at you, one after the other! The banners say, "Welcome to our home", and "We are serving all of your favorite foods!" and "Our dining chairs are so luxurious you will enjoy having this meal with us!" Moreover, your host is shouting these same things so there is no chance of your missing their intention to treat you like royalty.

Suddenly, you don't feel very good about your decision to accept this dinner invitation. Still, you brace yourself for the evening, mustering all the positivity you can. What you don't realize is there are more surprises in store for you. Your host then proceeds to entertain you by trying to talk about random things *they* think might interest you. They won't let you change the topic and don't ask your opinion on anything. As you are trying to take it all in, they insist on giving you a tour of the house. You look around, trying to figure out how or why you are made to peek into bedrooms, bathrooms and storerooms. After this grueling ordeal, dinner is served, but the host insists on serving one course after the other in quick succession. There's music playing somewhere, the television screen in the corner has a movie playing, and the host is trying to amuse you with some interesting anecdotes. The food is excellent, but the courses come and go so quickly, you are barely able to appreciate each one, however, you have already lost your appetite due to all the things you have been made to tolerate in the name of hospitality. Finally, the dinner comes to an end and you leave feeling a bit dazed.

TRUE CONNECTIONS

A couple of weeks after this disastrous dinner, the host calls you up and suggests you come visit for lunch. This time, you politely decline, citing other engagements.

So, what went wrong here? Your host had the best intentions when they tried to entertain you but, it was all too much and too loud to be considered entertaining. The food was good, but the other things completely ruined your experience and the result is you would probably do everything in your power to avoid going to this person's house again!

You can see the above scenario is obviously exaggerated. No sane person would behave that way with guests because that's just stupid, but that is exactly how a lot of websites treat their visitors.

It is baffling how many marketers are out of touch with what an audience needs. Below are a few things that you should get rid of immediately:

1. **Moving banners**
   When moving banners, or sliders, first became popular in the online world, many web designers wanted to incorporate this cool new feature on their website. It was thought to be an effective way to display the different categories of products and services in one shot. So, rotating banners ruled website design until someone tested its effectiveness. It was found rotating banners reduced conversions by 10-15%. They distract the user and eat into their already low concentration levels. As a result, the users never get around to browsing the website properly. Also, visitors are seldom interested in knowing about everything you have to offer. They are more interested in what they want. So, as a rule, avoid moving banners.

2. **Colorful websites**
   Using color is good until you use so many it borders on launching an assault on the visitors' eyes. Too many colors, or colors that are too bright, make for a very bad user experience. They don't help in *beautifying* the website as some designers might think. Instead, you should stick to using only 2-3 color palettes. Use colors wisely

to make the CTA and other important links stand out. Choose a text color that can be easily read. Bright colors could be used on websites that supply toys or other businesses of that nature, but it's important to know where to draw the line.

3. **Inconsistency**
   You need to be consistent with the design throughout your website. So, if your *Buy* button is blue on one page, it shouldn't be red on another. If you choose one font for the product descriptions in one category, don't use a completely different font on the other categories. When users are absorbed in browsing a website, their brains automatically latch on to consistent design aspects. This is how they can distinguish between various buttons such as *Submit, Add to Cart, Next Page*, etc., almost without having to read what's written. This *auto-pilot mode*, which enables users to act without having to think too much, is great for conversions. Any inconsistencies standing out make users unfocused. They cannot connect with the website and it causes confusion and hesitation while moving down the conversion path.

4. **Distracting ads**
   Sponsored ads that move are another bad idea. There are only two outcomes here: the attraction towards the movement of the ad is so much the user clicks on it and forgets your website; or the user gets so annoyed by the constant animation they close the webpage. Either case, there's no winning here.

5. **Animation**
   Many websites think it's a great idea to have their discount offers and any other information constantly flashing on the page. They think this is the best way to make sure visitors don't miss it but, honestly, there is nothing better than this to give the visitors a headache and send them away from the website.

There are other, much better ways to acquaint your visitors with the offers and discounts.

6. **Banner ads**

   There was a time when creating banner ads and placing them on other websites was a good strategy. In recent times, however, users have become immune to the charms of banner ads and adept at ignoring them completely. Media rich ads and other more effective ways of advertising have taken over.

The six items discussed above need to be completely removed from your website. Now, let's discuss some things marketers should consider ensuring they are not falling into the trap of making stupid and selfish mistakes.

1. **Chat boxes**

   Using chat boxes is a good way to make your website interactive, but chat boxes that appear the moment a visitor lands on your page are more distracting than helpful.

   When the visitor first visits your website, give them some time to experience it. If you think they have been on the page for a while without doing anything, help them along with a chat box. That way, you don't get in the way of the user's feel for the website. The chat box on *Agoda.com* is launched if the user has been on the page for some time without taking any action. It's helpful while still being non-intrusive.

2. **Error messages**

   It's a given that at some time or another, users will make mistakes whenever they are required to type something on a website. It could be a coupon code, search string, or even the name of the city they live in, mistakes are normal, and they happen quite a lot. What is not acceptable though, is your website admonishing the user for making a mistake.

   The impersonal message *This field is required* is like their high school teacher telling them they gave a wrong answer on a test. Be gentler. Tell them why you need this information.

If the search string entered has a typing error, or it does not exactly match anything you have on your website, don't give them a cold *No results* message. Instead, re-direct them to the results page that is most closely related to the entered search string, or auto correct the misspelling to give them the best search results.

Some websites are so focused on getting the information they need from the users they forget to help the users give this information correctly. The result is vague error messages, which don't tell the users exactly what is wrong.

3. **Surveys**

    Surveys are good tools to get to know your audience better. If you have visitors and customers filling out survey forms for you, you can use the information collected to boost your conversions. But, when it comes to the people who need to fill out these forms, they are not aware of the significance of this information. Even though a marketer might be tempted to get the survey launched as soon as possible, the visitor will not appreciate being disturbed during an active search. Surveys should never be launched before the visitor has had the time to visit at least 3-5 pages. It would be even better if the survey the visitors are requested to take would display when they are ready to exit the website.

4. **Discount pop-ups**

    A marketer wants to offer visitors a discount to entice them into making a purchase. A greedy marketer can't wait to offer the discount. A hasty and conditional promise of a discount is something visitors will not like very much. Never force the visitor to subscribe in order to get a discount, or have the pop-up come even before a visitor can figure out whether the website has the products they want. What good is a discount if you don't have what the visitor needs?

TRUE CONNECTIONS

5. **Forcing registrations**
   Many websites force visitors to register on the website. Want a discount? Register first! Did you come here for a free download? Register first! Looking for content? Register first!

   If you think this is a clever way to get registrations and generate leads, you're wrong. It's downright annoying, and in some cases, it's equivalent to cheating. You simply cannot force a visitor to register before you give them what you promised. Now, if you were to first give them the discount code, the download, or the content they came for, then you could ask them whether they would like to register to get more of it. This would make a world of difference!

6. **Shaming the users for not choosing to convert**
   As if forcing registrations on visitors wasn't bad enough, some marketers go even further to make users uncomfortable.

   There are many websites where users are given two options: they either sign-up or *admit that they'd rather not save money!*

   Or, a pop-up box from *Grammarly.com*. It's telling you if you don't get their tool, you're okay with making writing errors.

   Or House Beautiful wants people to join their email list or declare they like a decrepit house.

   Why would marketers want to bully or shame people into doing something because they feel it is good for their business? Unfortunately, the internet is full of examples like those described above.

7. **Slow webpages**
   At one time or another, you all have visited a website that loads at an agonizingly slow pace. As new pictures load, the text keeps moving down as you try to read it. The result is you finally decide whatever treasures the website holds are not worth the time it is taking to reveal them. Design your website so it loads faster. Studies have shown the time it takes to load a webpage is directly

proportionate to the irritation it causes visitors. People simply do not have the time or patience to wait for a webpage to open. Faster websites keep everyone happy.

8. **Using wrong pictures**
   The importance of using appropriate pictures cannot be stressed enough. Misleading pictures, pictures misrepresenting the target group, or pictures that look downright pretentious or fake are a very bad idea for your website.

You should also check your website to see if it has the following irritating issues:

1. **No mobile optimization**
   If you don't think it is worth your time or money to get your website optimized for mobile devices, you're wrong. If you have a reasonable amount of online conversions, mobile optimization is a natural progression. If you ignore this very important customer need, you're looking at losing a lot of your customer base.

2. **Difficult navigation**
   Does your website have difficult navigation? If visitors must look for the navigation links on your homepage, you have a problem. If a visitor must look for ways to go back a couple of pages or has to start all over again from the homepage, you have a problem. Difficult navigation that requires people to think and read too much is frustrating for them. Instead, go for role-based navigation and use visual navigation wherever possible. It also helps to have *breadcrumbs* on your webpages to make it easier for visitors to move from page to page without difficulty.

   Even though visual navigation works well, if you have too many categories for visitors to choose from, it's just a mess.

3. **Difficult checkouts**
   The goal is to get your visitors to the checkout, but stupid website designs get in the way and ruin it. Many websites will try to

cross-sell when the visitor is ready to pay, or, the visitor is asked to register to the site in order to process the purchase. Some websites ask for too much information during the checkout. As a rule of thumb, when a customer is ready to pay, *let them give you their money!* Just stay out of the way and let them complete the checkout process. Any suggestions for buying more, feedback forms, etc. can and must wait.

4. **Too much text**

   You have a lot you want to say to your visitors, so you put lengthy text everywhere you can. Your intentions might be good, but the outcome is not. Have you considered visitors might not be interested in everything you want to tell them, or they don't have the time to read all the information? Unless you are a content-driven website, lengthy content needs to be replaced by short, easy to read, concise copy.

5. **Jargon**

   Jargon-laden copy that you find insightful could prove to be tedious for your readers. Use language that is easy to understand. If they come across text that is too technical and uninteresting to them, you are just boring them into leaving.

Memory Load and Marketing

Short term memory is already in small reserve, and if your website strains this reserve by making visitors use too much working memory, the results are usually not in your favor. So, unless your website is a place where people come to take memory tests, there is no justification for making them think too much.

Things like these that contribute to memory load need careful consideration and improvement:

- **Displaying more than ten product categories.**
  Users only end up getting confused if they are given too many choices. If trying to figure out where they need to go in order to get what they want is a job that requires too much thinking, they won't want any part of it.

- **Having different visual elements for similar options.**
  If the *Submit* button is different on each page, or if the *Next Page* button is on the bottom of one page, then moves to the top on another page, visitors constantly need to be on their toes. This *style* of designing does not support user-led intuitive navigation.

- **Not highlighting the links visited.**
  When there is a large website with many pages, it is asking too much if you expect visitors to remember which ones they have already looked at. Instead, help them by changing the color of the links to pages they have already been, so they don't feel like they are walking through a maze.

Jeopardizing the Website's Credibility

It takes a lot of effort to get visitors to trust you, but, make one little mistake, and that trust turns into skepticism. Avoid false claims and misinformation. Instead, under-promise and over-deliver. If you know your product takes 8-10 business days for delivery, don't claim to deliver in 5-7 business days. Also, if your telephone service isn't 24/7, mention the times during which the service is available and make sure the number works! There's nothing like a dead telephone number to make potential customers back off. Imagine the panic attack a customer will have when they make a high dollar purchase, only to find out the phone number for tracking the purchase is out of order. The same goes for chat services.

Mishandling Reviews

Reviews are an essential part of e-commerce websites. For people who are looking to buy something from a website, customer reviews are important. They let others know the business has satisfied customers. If the reviews from previous customers are great, half the marketing for those products is already done. But what if reviews are bad?

When it comes to online reviews, it is a bad strategy to get defensive when a customer says the product is bad. Arguing with a dissatisfied customer to try to prove a point might win you an argument, but you will lose the customer you're arguing with and you will also lose the respect and trust of anyone reading this *war of words* on your website.

As Dale Carnegie said, the only way to get the best of an argument is to avoid it. So, how about graciously accepting your mistake and offering to help the customer? If the customer accepts your resolution, all is well but, if they are too angry for you to pacify them, at least others looking at the reviews will see the effort you made. They will know that you take customer satisfaction seriously and trust you more when they see you're fighting a difficult situation.

The same applies to the company's social media. Social media easily becomes a battleground for groups of people who simply happen to have different opinions and engage in passionate debates that can sometimes get out of hand. Dealing with criticism with as much grace as you deal with praise is an important quality, which needs to be seen by your audience.

Conclusion

Sometimes, marketers realize their website isn't doing what it should ideally do: consistently win conversions. This is when they resort to stupid tricks in order to somehow achieve CRO. The problem is, tricks don't help; good, well-thought out strategies do. However, strategic changes in the website are easier said than done. They need time, money and patience. If you can't make strategic changes in the website design right away, use tactical changes in the way your website and the peripheral system work. Just don't let your business fall prey to stupid tricks which will only ruin whatever good reputation your business already has.

ALL TOUCH POINTS

Customer touch points refer to every opportunity and interaction between the customer and any part of your business before, during, and after conversion. It is called a *touch point* because through every point (i.e. interaction), your aim is to *touch* the customer in some way, so the interaction has a positive impact on them. The objective is to enhance the user experience at every touch point, so the interaction is smooth and encourages the user to increase their involvement with the business. It could be something as small as noticing an ad about your brand, or something more involved, such as purchasing a product or service from your website.

Touch points are important and meaningful for marketing because they greatly influence buying decisions. How the customer feels at these touch points also impacts the relationship you want to build between the customer and the business. In order to understand the touch points, you must put yourself into the customer's shoes and look at things from their perspective. Touch points are all about user experience so, if you give enough thought to customer touch points, it can give your conversions a real boost.

Touch points are so powerful they can positively or negatively impact several important aspects of your business such as brand awareness, brand credibility, sales, customer retention, and of course, customer satisfaction. A positive experience will take the customer a long way towards brand preference. At the same time, a negative experience will not just affect the current conversion decision, it will also impact any future encounters the customer might have with the business.

But marketers need to understand whether a typical customer can perform key tasks on the website and assess the customer's emotional reaction to each point in the task completion process. Usability testing can give you the right idea about task completion rates and the user's response to each stage. Analytics and other testing used to determine how the website, or changes to it, affects the user can help evaluate the success of all touch points. Therefore, it would be a big help to create scenarios for each interaction so the process can be assessed from the customer's point of view.

Understanding Touch Points

Touch points make a huge difference in how users perceive your business. The user experience talked about so often is the collective effect of the user's reaction to each touch point. So, if you have designed an aesthetically pleasing website with a neat, internal search process, but your checkout pages are lengthy and not user-friendly, the user experience takes a hit. Similarly, if your website has all the elements to contribute towards a good user experience, but your online help center is anything but helpful, users seeking help would be dissatisfied.

All touch points work in tandem to ensure users have a good experience. They also influence brand perceptions, which stay with the users for a long time.

A positive approach is to look at touch points as opportunities to develop relationships between the users and the business. You can choose how to handle the users at each touch point, but as a good marketer, it is your responsibility to make the interaction at each touch point valuable and memorable for each user.

TRUE CONNECTIONS

Touch points can be broadly categorized into three phases in the marketing cycle: before, during, and after conversion.

Before Conversion

- Customer exposure to the brand through advertising or social media
- Visiting the homepage or landing page
- Reading content on the website
- Newsletters
- Using the search option within the website to look for something in particular
- Customer service through chat/phone
- FAQ pages
- Reviews, ratings, and testimonials
- Marketing emails

During Conversion

- Forms to be filled out
- Sign-ups and registrations
- Cart checkouts
- Payment methods
- Customer service through chat/phone

After Conversion

- Confirmation emails

- Follow up emails

- Packaging and delivery

- Cross-selling emails

- Emails about discounts and other offers

- Policies about returns or replacements

- Customer service through chat/phone

The next step is to map out the role-based path users follow, after the first touch point. Check to see if this path moves them towards user satisfaction or user dissatisfaction. Then, break up each touch point into tasks and run tests to see how easy or difficult it is for users to accomplish these tasks.

Usability testing is a good option to check what works, what needs improvement, and what needs to go.

Usability Tests

Usability tests give valuable insights into customers' online behavior, their reactions to tasks, the common mistakes, website pitfalls, etc. They can help identify areas needing improvement in the existing system or test any changes to the system. Even if your website is not quite ready, users can test a prototype.

When it can't be decided which features work, and which features are compromising system performance, usability tests help to give a definitive answer.

You don't need a large sampling to carry out these tests. You can start with a group of four or five users. Even this small number of users can help identify most damaging problems on a website. It would be a good idea to run the tests on this small group of participants, fix the problems they identify, then run the tests on another small group. This second group will further help to reveal any deeper problems. Fix these problems, then run the tests again. Repeat this until you have eliminated almost all major problems.

To get the best results from usability tests, they should be carried out regularly and not just when some changes are being introduced. Marketers might have reservations using these tests due to time and budget constraints, however, if you look closely, the tests are quite cost-effective and completely worth the resources they use. These tests can be used by small businesses as well as large enterprises and result in valuable findings.

Once you have the results from each phase of the usability test, try to figure out what you can do to make a more positive impression on the users at each point.

Customer Feedback

Customer feedback also gives you information about what is not working well for your business. Customers may choose to rate their experience and provide feedback on their own, or you could provide a survey for them to take. In both the cases, the customer is likely to reveal both major and minor pitfalls in the way you operate as a business.

The customer feedback should always be taken seriously. Even if you disagree with the customers' opinion, you can't ignore genuine feedback. If the customers say some features within your website need changes, or your packaging needs improvement, you need to look at things from their perspective and make changes wherever necessary.

Prospect Scenarios

A scenario is the basis of a visitor's interaction with the business. When you talk about a prospect scenario in terms of a website, it would extend to identifying the visitor role and intent on the site. The scenario is defined from a customer perspective, so, it's not about how the *marketer* views a role, it's about what the customers need and expect from the website. It's okay that the scenarios are not extensive, if they are able to identify and characterize the most common and important uses.

Look at this example:

Premise: An offline training center providing cognitive skills training specifically for children.

Scenario 1 – A mother wanting to know more about the training offered for her child who falls in the autism spectrum.

Scenario 2 – A father wanting to find out how the training would help his gifted daughter to enhance her skills through reviews from other parents.

Scenario 3 – A teacher interested in knowing whether the training could help some of her problem students who have difficulty paying attention in class.

Scenario 4 – A mother who wants to enroll her son after a friend's review that their daughter benefited greatly from the training.

All the above scenarios are about people who have a strong reason to explore the website. These scenarios can be simulated to identify all touch points and each prospect's reaction to them.

For example, if you look at the first scenario, the prospect is looking for information. She does not want to be redirected to a sales landing page with offers, nor does she want to know how it helped other children who might not have special needs like her own child. She wants to know about how the training would take place and how it would help improve her child's cognitive skills. After having these basic details, she would need further information about how the training works, the duration of the training, some information about the trainers, etc. If you were to break the main task of the prospect into specific subtasks, you would get something like this:

- Determine whether the training center is reliable

- Look at the various courses available and determine which is best suited for the prospect's needs

- Look at testimonials from parents of other special needs children

- Contact the helpline to get more information

Now, if you look at the fourth scenario, the mother in this case is already impressed by the effect of the training on her friend's daughter. She is already convinced the training works and interested in enrolling her son for the training. If you break her intent into subtasks, it will look something like this:

- Identify the closest training center

- Look at the pricing details

- Apply referral coupon for a discount in the training fees

- Make an appointment for a face-to-face discussion with the training coordinator

Based on the above two scenarios, it's clear two people visiting the same website might go through different touch points, but the common thread is they *will* base their decisions on the experience they have.

Touch Points Before Purchase

Advertising/Brand Introduction

Convincing ad copy, an authoritative proposition, and an impressive logo are the things people remember. These are just a few of the things a good ad should aim at for getting this touch point right.

Organic/Paid Search

Do you redirect the traffic to the correct landing page or microsite depending on their source and intent? The point at which visitors first come to your website or any part of it, is a very important touch point. It's a test for how well you have designed your webpages and customized the pages according to user needs.

Organic traffic – If you have organic traffic coming in from searches, make sure you give them exactly what they need according to the keywords used.

Paid searches/PPC - The rule that applies for organic searches also extends to paid searches. The users should get what they asked for – nothing more, nothing less.

Even when you make sure you send visitors to the correct landing page or microsite; the next question should be whether that page is optimized for customer satisfaction.

A few best practices are:

- Make sure the information is accurate and helpful
- Use trust symbols to make customers feel safe
- Use pictures visitors can relate to
- Unclutter the webpage so important information stands out

- Use visible and easily actionable CTA buttons

- Use role-based visual navigation

- Use colors and fonts appropriately

The first step to increasing sales and revenue on a website is to remove the barriers to conversion. Optimize your landing pages according to tested and proven principles of conversion-optimized landing pages, and you're well on your way to increasing your sales and revenue.

Product Category Pages

Products should be categorized under different headings depending on what visitors are looking for. To give a simple example, when a website sells books, people always come to the site looking for books by genre or author name, so have categories based on that. There is no point in having categories such as paperback and hardcover.

The product details should also clearly mention the features, pricing, customization (if available and/or applicable), shipping details, delivery timelines, return policies, etc.

Educational Pages

If your users land on informational pages while looking for educational content, they should be offered good quality, useful content. You could have subtle CTAs for conversion but, stick to giving as much information as possible. A content page that is pushy and focuses only on sales is off-putting and makes the website look selfish, which can't be a good touch point experience for the visitor.

Reviews and Ratings Pages

For most visitors, reviews from verified buyers looks like a safety net. If you have a large enough customer base, it always helps to use reviews and ratings written by them. However, perfect ratings are not possible in the real world so, don't worry about less than perfect ratings for your products. Don't let that odd bad review bother you. In fact, when new customers are looking at these reviews, it is proof your review system is honest and transparent.

Helpline (Chat/Call)

If visitors to a website need some human interaction to understand a feature, or ask a question, the support staff should be able to provide the correct information. They should also know what action to take if they don't know the correct answers. A chat or phone conversation with a staff member is a very impactful touch point that can make or break the customer experience.

Touch Points During Purchase

Cart Checkouts

Checkouts are a critical touchpoint since it not only impacts user experience, it can also make you forfeit the sale you are about to make. The customer selects products and adds them to the cart but, when they proceed to the checkout, they discover they have been charged an excessive amount for shipping and handling charges. Surprising your customer at the last minute is the worst mistake you could possibly make. If you want to surprise your customers, surprise them with good things such as a lucky draw coupon, or an instant discount.

Swift checkouts are also equally, if not more, important. Nobody wants to go through a lengthy a checkout process. A quick and easy checkout means less chance of cart abandonment. Discourage cart abandonments by using a pop-up if the customer tries to leave without completing the checkout.

Filling Out Forms

If you want customers to register on your website, wait until they have gone through the payment process before suggesting a sign-up. If it is necessary for you to have certain information before you confirm the order, make sure the form you ask them to fill out is as short and easy as possible. Lengthy forms, which seem to give error messages at the drop of a hat, are a very bad idea.

When a customer wants something from the website and they want it quickly, don't stand in their way by making it difficult for them to get to the product. Websites that don't get greedy and ask for sign-ups upfront are more likely to get sign-ups willingly after the purchase is complete.

Chat/Call Helpline (Pre-Purchase)

If a customer requires support for a problem during or immediately after a purchase, the support staff should be equipped to handle the problem. They should realize the caller is very close to making a purchase, but there is something causing a delay that could cause them to feel frustrated and lost. A caring approach and a genuine will to help the customer will result in a good experience for the caller.

Touch Points After Purchase

Transactional Emails

Once the customer has gone through with the purchase, send them an email acknowledging their order. Next, send them an e-invoice and reiterate the shipping/delivery timeline. Once the order ships, give them tracking details. Make sure this crucial post-purchase touch point counts.

Cross-Selling Emails

Cross-selling emails can be used for more than just selling; they can be used to deepen the customers' connection with the brand. If you want to expose your customers to related products, or products that complement the products they already bought, now is a good time. Only, make sure the emails are not too frequent, and are always about relevant products.

Handling Reviews

Customer reviews could be either on your website or independent review websites. Customers who decide to leave a review give an opportunity for another touch point.

Encourage your customers to rate and review the products they have bought. If they are happy with the product and leave a good review, acknowledge the review and thank them. But, be prepared for angry, dissatisfied customers and their bad reviews. Of course, you should take every care to ensure quality products and timely delivery but, the truth is, you will still have customers who are not happy. When an irate customer decides to vent in a review, they do not hold back so, be prepared to take the heat. Remember there is no winning when it comes to an argument with a customer, even if you are right. So, the best way is to not start an argument.

Instead, work on calming the customer by providing a solution to their problem. *Delayed delivery?* Apologize. *Wrong product delivered?* Apologize, then offer a return or replacement. *Customer received a damaged product.* Apologize, then let them choose between a refund and a replacement. Notice in all these examples an apology is the first thing you should do? An apology goes a long way.

If you are lucky, the customer will be happy with the solutions you offer them. Even if none of your solutions are acceptable, other customers will see that instead of getting into an ugly war of words with the customer, you owned up, took responsibility, and tried to help.

Chat/Call Helpline (Post-Purchase)

If customers need to call the helpline or use the chat option to ask about delayed deliveries, the support staff should be able to obtain the tracking information for them. If they have a complaint regarding the product or the packaging, the support person should be well equipped to handle the issues calmly and professionally and correct them in any way possible.

If you have a ticket system to address customer issues, it is important to make sure every interaction with the customer is handled with care. Instead of hurrying to close out the tickets, emphasis should be placed on providing real solutions to the customers.

Packaging and Delivery

If your website sells products, does your delivery system guarantee the product reaches the customer within the promised time frame? Any delays will lead to frustration and lack of trust and usually end in a bad review online and/or an earful for the support staff on call.

If the delivery is received when expected, it really doesn't do much good if the product is damaged during shipping. Good, sturdy, packaging protecting the product is very important. Also, don't forget to add instructions on how to use the product, a paper invoice/receipt and coupons to be used for future purchases to the package. A *thank you* note would also be a very nice touch.

How Should You Treat Returning Customers?

If you have customers that come back to you, how do you treat them? Do you acknowledge they are existing customers and make them feel special and appreciated? Or do you make them go through the same steps as a new visitor?

Repeat customers are an asset to your business and it simply won't do to ignore their significance. For repeat customers visiting your website, the touch point has even more importance. This is because they come with some expectations and beliefs.

The effect of having the sign-in panel for existing users first is two-fold.

1. The repeat customers sense you care about them by visually giving them first preference.

2. New users see this and the fact that you have repeat customers is acknowledged. You provide social proof and encouragement for the new user to register.

Involving the Staff

Your company's staff should be given adequate training to help them understand how the business works. Their involvement in every effort towards customer satisfaction should be encouraged and they should be held accountable for all the touch points within their departments. By distributing responsibility towards customer relationships at various levels, you can ensure all bases are covered.

Good customer feedback should be shared with all the staff so the importance of keeping customers happy and satisfied at each point can be demonstrated.

In Conclusion

Good relationships with customers depend upon how good an experience they have when they do business with your company. By optimizing user experience at all touch points, you are making sure all bases are covered. A tight, closely monitored strategy to ensure your customers always have something good to say about your business is a definite step towards establishing a real connection with them.

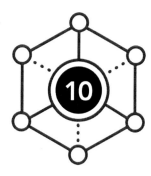

CREATING FANS

Companies spend considerable resources for customer acquisition and they constantly monitor the cost per acquisition and the average value per acquisition to ensure the ROI is good. But, if companies were to look at the benefits of customer retention in the same way, the returns could be significantly higher.

For example, if a website has acquired 100 customers in a month, and the cost per acquisition is $10, the company spends $1,000 on customer acquisition. If the average order value per customer is $100, the company manages to earn a revenue of $10,000, making the profit margin $9,000.

Now, if the company manages to get 50 out of the initial 100 customers to buy from them again, the customer acquisition cost in this case is $0, since these 50 customers have already made purchases on the website. When these customers buy from the website again, the profit margin increases.

In the above example, you have only considered the customer acquisition cost. There would also be customer retention costs involved. However, the cost, as well as the effort required for customer retention, would be lower than bringing in new customers.

This does not mean *all* your efforts should be redirected to customer retention once you have a good customer base. Every business needs a constant supply of new customers in order to thrive, but you can't ignore the benefits of having returning customers.

Aside from the fact that having returning customers helps increase the financial returns, these customers also help market your product by word-of-mouth. In the long run, they are also more likely to form a good relationship with the business. This increases their lifetime value for the business.

Lifetime Value of the Customers

The lifetime value (LTV) of a customer is the net profit a business can make from current as well as future transactions with a customer. So, if a customer returns to the website several times, or makes high-value purchases, their lifetime value increases.

Customer Satisfaction, Loyalty, and Lifetime Value

What encourages people to remain loyal to your brand and continue being valuable customers?

Marketing experts have observed four (4) important factors that influence customer retention and brand loyalty. These are: 1) customer satisfaction level, 2) strength of relationship, 3) switching costs, and 4) attractiveness of alternatives. Let's go into more detail:

1. **Satisfaction with products and services**
   Customer satisfaction and retention are closely linked. When customers recognize the products and services they are getting meet or exceed their expectations, they will believe they are getting good value for the price they've paid. This increases the likelihood they will reorder these products or services from the same company or brand. If their individual circumstances and purchase situation does not change, and they continue to buy the product from the

same brand, over time, they will develop a preference for it. This increases their loyalty to the company or brand.

On the other hand, if customers feel they are not getting good value for their money, sooner or later they will start looking for an alternative. But, as you will see below, while customer satisfaction is significant, it is not the only factor that can influence the decision to remain a customer.

2. **Strength of the relationship with the company/brand**
The customer's relationship with the company or brand also influences their level of loyalty to the company's products or services. Buyer and seller relationships typically fall under two categories: 1) pure transactional and 2) relational exchange.

Pure transactional relationships are low in commitment. The customer primarily buys products based on price and is frequently switching between different sellers. This is usually the case with business-to-consumer businesses where customers tend to buy products from competing brands, except when they have developed a certain preference for particular brands (most likely household names), or when they have specific requirements that can only be fulfilled by a certain company or brand.

On the other hand, relational exchange relationships are characterized by a higher level of commitment between the buyer and the seller. The customer and company/brand develop a long-term relationship as they continue to connect over a period. Through a series of transactions, both parties establish trust and some level of dependence on each other. This can be seen in most business-to-business (or B2B) transactions, wherein the customer relies on the seller to supply some sort of product or service in a certain amount of time, while the seller commits to delivering the expected quality and quantity of product/service to the customer for as long as they are both in the business relationship.

It's safe to assume relational exchange relationships increase customer loyalty as opposed to purely transactional ones. Because of the length of the relationship and the amount of resources that have been devoted to establishing it, the stakes are higher for both the customer and the company. The deeper the relationship with the company or brand, the deeper the commitment and loyalty of both parties.

3. **Switching costs**

   The cost involved in switching to another brand or company is an important factor when it comes to customer loyalty because switching can be costly to the customer. They stand to lose something once they decide to change providers and these costs occur at different stages in the customer's decision-making process.

First, there are pre-switching costs involved during the search and evaluation phase of the customer's decision to change. Customers must spend time and effort when they research information and evaluate available options that can possibly replace their current brand or company. Then there is the psychological uncertainty they will experience with regards to the performance of a new and untested brand, company, or provider.

Next are the set-up costs required to successfully initiate the switch. This also involves time and effort on the part of the customer. When set-up costs are low, then there is little to discourage customers from beginning a relationship with a new brand, company, or provider. For example, when it comes to common household products, a customer can simply pick a new product off the shelf and use it the same way they did the old one.

Lastly, there are the post-switching costs associated with acquiring and adapting to the features of the new product or brand. For instance, some products and services, such as software or hardware, require a learning curve for the customer to use them successfully. This can discourage customers from frequently changing the software or equipment they use since they are already familiar with, or may even be experts at, their current software or equipment.

Switching costs are usually lower for very common products, such as household items, but it's a different story for high ticket purchases or products and services compelling customers to somehow enter a personal exchange, such as a postpaid mobile or internet subscription. Here, the pre-switching costs are higher as customers are exposed to risks in terms of trustworthiness, dependability, and reliability of the alternatives. In the case of B2B contracts, the customer can also lose some of the economic and non-economic benefits from their long-term contractual arrangement with a company or provider, or even pay a fee for terminating their contract early.

This is how switching costs can encourage customers to remain loyal to a brand/company even when they are dissatisfied with the product or service. If the benefits of staying with the current product, brand, or company is seen to outweigh the costs of changing to a new one, then it is very unlikely the customer will be making the switch soon.

4. **Attractiveness of alternatives**

   The presence of attractive alternatives in the market is a major factor in customers' decisions to switch from a product or brand. If competitors have better offers or present products that are significantly less expensive, this could influence customers to consider switching from the product or brand they currently use. This is especially true for products or services where there is little to no difference in price or quality. In this case, your brand or company must be able to provide a unique and valued service that would be difficult to match by your competitors.

   In order to attract customer attention and trigger desire, the alternative brand must be significantly better in quality by customers. If there is no significant difference, they will not have a strong desire to switch. This means the threat of customers switching is reduced when customers are highly satisfied with their existing product or service and will be more likely to want to continue being valuable customers to your business.

Ensuring high levels of customer satisfaction, establishing a strong relationship with your customers, and providing them with great offers can increase customer commitment, increase switching costs, and make customers uninterested in alternatives. Customers who are satisfied with your products and services are also more likely to remain loyal to your brand or company, and they will reward your commitment to quality with valuable repeat business for a long time.

Building Customer Loyalty and Lifetime Value in the Online World

Understanding the factors that drive customer loyalty and lifetime value is useful in your efforts to keep customers and increase the value they bring to your company. This knowledge can help you plan the best strategy for ensuring you deliver good and consistent quality to your customers. Also, it gives you a basis for evaluating your company's approach and actual practices for customer retention and encouraging repeat purchases.

What Makes Customers Return?

Having a loyal customer base who repeatedly purchase from you gives you an important competitive advantage in the world of e-commerce. It can help reduce marketing costs, build brand equity, and boost overall business performance. But in order to cultivate loyalty among your online customers, you must first be able to encourage repeat visits and purchases.

Which brings you to an important question: What makes customers return to your website?

TRUE CONNECTIONS

1. **The customer has a very good user experience on the website.**
   Studies confirm that a user-friendly website and a good user experience are important if you want customers to make purchases and keep coming back to your site. Ease of use, trustworthiness and clarity rank high among online users' criteria for visiting and conducting transactions on a website. In a research on the fundamentals of consumers' repeat online buying of groceries published in *The International Review of Retail, Distribution and Consumer Research*, Torben Hansen (2006) observed complicated websites discourage consumers from repeat online purchases. Another study conducted by Veronika Masínová and Zuzana Svandová (2014) showed a web design with clear navigation and information, influenced not only visitors' impressions of the professionalism of the website but also their decision to buy from that e-commerce site.

2. **The purchase gives them a good value for the money spent.**
   Like any customer, online buyers want their purchases to be worth every penny they spend. This means buyers expect the product or service they just bought to meet their needs and fulfill whatever claims were made. Otherwise, they are likely to experience buyer's regret in making the decision to purchase. To prevent this, you need to make sure you have clear and accurate descriptions on your product detail pages. This includes high-quality images allowing online visitors see products in as much detail as possible. This way, they can determine if the product meets their requirements before they decide to buy it.

3. **They are very happy with the quality of the product/services they have purchased.**
   Product or service quality influences the way buyers think about value. When buyers recognize they are getting a product or service of superior quality, they are more likely to feel the price is worth it and be happy with their purchase. This increases brand/company loyalty. A study by Karin Venetis and Pervez Ghauri (2004) suggests a company's ability to deliver levels of high quality to

customers is the first and most important step in establishing trust and building a relationship with them. Once customers feel the brand or company is committed to providing them with excellent service, they are more inclined to want to stay on as long term. As a bonus, happy customers are more inclined to share their positive experience with others and influence their peers to buy the same product.

4. **The customer service provided is excellent.**
   Providing excellent customer service is crucial to the experience of your online buyers. Your ability to deliver timely and relevant communications to customers has a huge impact on their future buying decisions. You need to make sure all the messages you send to them create and reinforce their feeling of being valued by your company. From your online chat, pre- and post-purchase messages and packaging, you must focus on aligning your touch points, so they work together to deliver a personalized, smooth and exceptional customer experience. Consider every communication you have with your customers as an opportunity to make them feel special and reassure them they will be taken care of on every step of their purchase journey.

5. **The website has something unique to offer that isn't available elsewhere.**
   Achieving distinction is one of the hardest things for an online business because of the ease of entry in this industry. There are literally thousands of potential websites that visitors can land on for any given product. Most of them look and feel as if they were designed from the same template. So, if you want to stand out, you should avoid going the same generic route. This does not mean going crazy on your design and standards, which would most likely result in poor usability and confused visitors. Your goal should be that you provide visitors with the best user experience as possible. Use the tools discussed in the previous chapters to find out what your visitors need and give them a stress-free and fun experiences. You can create distinction for your website by

providing value-added services that delight online buyers. Your products may not be unique, but that doesn't mean you can't make the experience of buying your products memorable when you provide a high level of attention, such as personalized notes or special product packaging.

The good news is all the above points are within your control. You only must make a conscious decision to deliver on these points. If the last point is applicable to your business, you are in a very good position to use it to increase the LTV of a customer. However, remember being able to provide something exclusive only has a temporary benefit. Sooner or later, somebody else is going to come up with an idea to provide the customers with the same thing with a better approach.

How Can You Influence the LTV of a Customer?

Here are some things you can do to increase customer LTV:

1. Understand what customers need and provide it to them in an easy-to-buy way

2. Enhance the website experience to boost conversions

3. Build and maintain trust between the business and the customer

4. Take care of all touch points before and after customer contact with the website to ensure continued customer satisfaction

5. Put as much, if not more, effort into customer retention as you would into customer acquisition

Know your Customers

Understand your customer target group and know what they need. It's not only about the products or services they need, it's also about how their needs are met.

Identify which customers are first-time buyers or repeat buyers. You want to focus on first-time buyers to re-engage them with your business after the purchase and repeat customers to further deepen their commitment with the business, so they keep coming back.

The idea here is to constantly second guess what the customer may want and then make it available to them. Usability tests, surveys, feedbacks, etc. can help you to accurately determine customer needs.

Build and Maintain Trust

Trust plays a major role in customer retention. The fact that a customer has already purchased from you indicates the initial level of trust is already in place. However, they need assurances and cues from you to keep that trust going. For instance, completely ignoring their existence after they've given you their money would be a bad move that would destroy the trust you managed to build during the acquisition phase.

Give a Great Website Experience

As explained in previous chapters, a great website experience depends on a lot of things. A website that's merely usable doesn't make for a great experience. A website that is truly tuned in to the customer's requirements and helps them complete a task is what would give them a great experience.

Take Care of Touch Points Before and After Connection to the Website

This involves all contact including advertising, promotional and follow-up emails, cold calls, customer service, shipping and deliveries, return policies, etc. Who doesn't like some extra attention? If you keep all your communication relevant, personalized, and in moderation, customers will be willing to return to the website often.

Take Customer Retention Seriously

At first glance, it might seem that customer retention is a by-product of doing everything else right. While this is true to some extent, there's a lot more than that to customer retention. You need specific efforts to keep customers returning to the website. Some of these efforts include:

- **Encourage return visits**
  You can get customers to visit again by giving them something to look forward to such as an exclusive offer for repeat customers or early entry to an online sale or points they can redeem.

  Make them aware of new products that are related to their purchases, so they know where to go if they want to buy them.

  E-commerce websites can have a separate section for regular deals or contests, so customers are encouraged to drop in regularly to see what's new.

- **Make return visits easy**
  Help customers sign-in quickly and save their previous searches, purchases, shipping details, etc. to ensure a smooth and quick checkout.

  Save their preferences to make navigation to the right web pages easy.

- **Give incentives to returning customers and for referring new customers**
  If you want customers to return to your website and refer you to their friends, give them some motivation. For example, a privilege that can be unlocked only by existing customers, or a referral bonus when someone they refer makes a purchase.

- **Take customer feedback seriously**
  If you have returning customers giving you negative feedback about something on your website or any process involved, take it seriously. The same applies to surveys customers take. Change the

design, enhance features, remove bugs, and simplify the process. Once you do this, acknowledge the customers' contribution in bringing these issues to your attention and thank them for it.

- **Offer premium services**
  When you have customers who keep coming back, offer them a free upgrade to access premium services on your website. You can have a target based on a combination of number of return visits and money spent to select customers for an upgrade.

- **Give the customers something above and beyond what is expected**
  Perks don't always need to be in the form of monetary discounts. You can also give customers some extra features, resources, content, etc. What you need is something to distinguish you from your competitors.

- **Don't compromise on quality**
  Make sure whatever you offer to your buyers is of the best quality possible. Make sure they get value out of every cent they pay you. Take people's money seriously.

Segment Your Retention Efforts

One size does not fit all, so don't go down that road. Customize all your communications depending on the level of each customer's commitment to your brand. This means different promotional emails to new and returning buyers. Also, different emails to customers with low-value orders and high-value orders. Basically, use all the data you have on customers and segment them into practical groups until you can be sure every interaction with existing customers is as personalized as possible.

Create Fans

You have one-time buyers who buy just once and then disappear, then you have returning customers who always manage to find their way back to you for their purchases. Then, you have fans. Fans are invaluable to your business because they don't just add to your revenue by buying from you, they set a series of events into motion ultimately helping your business in more ways than one. They *always* buy from you, they trust you implicitly, they recommend you to everybody, and they say good things about you on social media and other open forums. Fans turn your business into a recognized brand. Creating fans goes beyond just retaining customers.

Turning Customers into Fans: The Virgin Airlines Story

Virgin America flew its last flight in 2018, but not before shaking up the airline industry.

Founded in 2004, Virgin America started operations in 2007 with the vision of bringing fun back into airline travel. At that time, the fiercely competitive industry was dominated on one hand by airline behemoths, and on the other hand, there were low-cost airlines that focused primarily on aggressive cost-cutting to offer lower fares. Founder Richard Branson wanted Virgin America to be the "fun, irreverent airline" delivering exceptional customer service rather than competing based on cost.

By distinguishing itself with a strong orientation towards quality service, Virgin America successfully carved its own niche in an already crowded market.

Exactly how did Virgin America accomplish this? Here are just some of the ways:

Prioritizing customer needs

Virgin America broke into the competitive airline industry by responding to the huge gap existing between customer expectations and the poor experience most airline passengers went through. The company's commitment to addressing passengers' inflight needs led to excellent levels of customer satisfaction, which was a considerable feat considering the widespread dissatisfaction that impacted the entire industry. Virgin America implemented several innovations based on what customers, as well as their own employees, wanted from air travel. For instance, the company fitted its airplanes with *mood lighting* and leather seats to make flying more comfortable. It also introduced on-demand food, a seat-back entertainment system, and pioneered the provision of in-flight wi-fi and *Netflix in the sky*.

Virgin America's focus on its customers was not only evident in its planes. It made sure customers could easily reach the airline contact center through different channels, whether by phone, email, social media or chat, and that messages were responded to within moments in a friendly and helpful manner.

Creating great customer experiences

Virgin America's efforts at learning about what air travelers wanted and then giving it to them allowed the company to build the experience the brand would become known for: fun, exciting, and delightful. Not a lot of airlines can do what Virgin America did: give its passengers experiences that went beyond just flying to a destination, but by connecting with their lives. For instance, the company created a "Here on Biz" app that let business-minded passengers meet other passengers who shared their interests. Their #FlyPE Free Ad Space contest also encouraged customers to share their own stories on how Virgin America's Premium Economy helped them with their business. The company also prepared exciting surprises for its passengers, like a primed flash mob of Motown the Musical cast on one of its Detroit flights.

By intentionally taking steps to create a remarkable experience for customers, Virgin America also inspired customers to tell others about their flying experience. Perhaps no other airline brand has been as shared on social media as Virgin America, which is a testament to the company's ability to deliver experiences that are worth talking to friends, family and colleagues about.

Empowering frontline employees

Frontline staff are an important touchpoint for airline passengers, and Virgin America made sure their customer-facing employees were empowered to take the initiative to always surprise and delight customers.

The crew were also given as much leeway to make decisions improving the customer experience. For instance, it wasn't uncommon on a Virgin America flight for a passenger to be bumped up from economy to a better class if they encountered problems with something even as simple as a broken in-flight screen. The Virgin America crew developed a culture for taking care of customers even in small, simple details. For instance, if there was a fantastic view outside, the flight crew would put a message up on the in-flight screen to encourage customers to look out the window so they would not miss it.

An airline brand that travelers would miss

Virgin America customers were unsurprisingly saddened and dismayed over the merger with Alaska Airlines and the latter's decision to discontinue the brand. But then, Virgin America had already shown other brands the no-fail strategy to create lifelong fans: focus on knowing your customers, deliver relevant and terrific experiences across touchpoints, and empower employees to make decisions that can lead to better customer experiences. This is how Virgin America interrupted the airline industry's notion of business travel and captured the hearts of air passengers.

What is the lesson here? Fans are not created overnight. Creating fans involves over-delivering on what is expected of you. For example, if a loyal customer buys a product from you and you deliver it on time, you haven't done anything extraordinary. Sure, they are satisfied, but that's exactly what is expected. But what if you consider they have been a regular customer and offer a free upgrade to express delivery to get the package delivered sooner than expected. How would that make the customer feel? Valued.

As you may have gathered from Virgin America's case, creating fans requires a concerted effort to ensure a smooth and consistent experience across all customer touchpoints. Any gap or inconsistency in the experience delivered by even just one of your touchpoints could result in a crack to the brand or company image from a customer viewpoint. If you want to turn customers into fans like Virgin America did, you need to start paying more attention to **ALL** your touchpoints.

Building a Fan Base by Optimizing for Customer Lifetime Value

Having loyal, committed fans is a holy grail for marketers. Brand and product fans are willing to go beyond just being customers. They are advocates who will defend the brand against bashers and non-believers and spread good information about the brand and its products. They are revenue drivers who will repeatedly choose to purchase your brand and products over others. But, as you have seen from the Virgin America example, you simply cannot grow a community of loyal fans if you are not willing to invest the time, effort, and other resources in order to gain your customers' love.

Strive to Surprise and Delight Customers

I once ordered from a new website dealing in kids' clothing. With my first order, they sent me a handwritten thank-you note from the founders. I loved that they took the time and stopped to acknowledge a new customer.

Not too many companies pay enough attention to making surprising and pleasant experiences for their customers. Most are content with meeting the bare minimum of customer expectations. But creating special experiences doesn't need to be expensive. For instance, if you're a small hotel, you don't have to go the Ritz Carlton way and fly someone across the country to deliver allergy-friendly food for a distraught customer. Even small gestures can go a long way in endearing your brand to your customers. Giving them a bottle of wine with a personal note or remembering their favorite menu item or special requests from their last visit will go a long way if these gestures are sincere.

On the flip side, there are companies attempting to stage surprise and wonderful moments for their customers just for the sake of media attention. This may work for a short while but, if pleasing customers isn't built into the core of your brand, it will soon be exposed as fraud by your own customers. Think about the many companies that tried to *greenwash* their brands in order to attract eco-conscious consumers, only to have their claims shown to be false.

Reward Customer Loyalty

Many companies reward customer loyalty by having a loyalty program in place. This is where customers rack up points for every purchase they make and then get to exchange the earned points for cash equivalents, discounts, or tangible items. You can see similar efforts in e-commerce, with numerous sites encouraging customers to continue purchasing through rewards programs. One of these companies is children's clothing retailer TheChildrensPlace.com. It has *MyPlaceRewards*, which allows its members to earn a point for each dollar spent in the online store. Members can then claim $5 for every 100 points they have accumulated. They also get access to exclusive offers such as birthday discounts and bonus events.

Your loyalty program does not have to be all about discounts. Beauty product retailer *Sephora.com*'s Beauty Insider loyalty program allows members to exchange their points for full-size samples or limited-edition releases of beauty products. They also encourage their Insider Community members to connect with each other and discuss their favorite products.

Improve Your Tech Support or Helpline

Don't underestimate the power your customer helpline holds in creating fans for your business. This very human interaction can make or break the image of your business in the eyes of a customer. Customer support staff who give generic answers to inquiries, often lack the training to deal with irate customers, and don't have the ability to come up with satisfactory resolutions lead to highly dissatisfied customers. Understand that customers come to the support team with their problems and if the staff can't solve their problems, which adds to their frustration, they are never coming back.

Good customer service reps know how to identify with customers and offer solutions. They aren't eager to close the ticket. Rather, they are more focused on solving the problem at hand to the best of their ability and to the point where customers are satisfied. But how good or bad your customer service reps perform ultimately depends on how empowered they are to use resources to help customers resolve and address any problem or difficulty encountered. If the reps, or any of your other employees, feel powerless and dissatisfied at work, this will weaken their ability to assist customers and reflect badly on your brand.

Actively Encourage Feedback and Word of Mouth

Word-of-mouth (WOM) is a powerful trust-builder and helps you acquire more customers. There is a concept in psychology suggesting you should actively encourage WOM from your customers if you want to strengthen their loyalty to your brand. This is known as Confirmation Bias, or, the tendency to favor and recall information in a way confirming one's preexisting beliefs. By asking your customers to become spokespeople of your brand's message, you not only get word out about your products and services, you also turn more of your loyal customers into active fans.

In this situation, you should not wait until customers have become repeat purchasers to ask them to become a brand spokesperson. With the right nudge, you can convince visitors who have recently made a purchase to spread word about their experience. You can consider giving incentives for referrals to motivate your customers to invite their friends and family members to try your products.

People usually give feedback and share their experiences only when they are highly motivated, either positively or negatively. It's up to you to ensure your customers will only talk about your brand in a positive manner, and the negative rants, reviews and feedback that are posted about you are turned into opportunities to recover a dissatisfied customer or, even possibly create more fans in the process or reinforcing the brand's message.

Conclusion

Fans are not created overnight. They result from multiple positive encounters your customers have with your brand touchpoints. The key thing to remember is your brand must be able to consistently provide

TRUE CONNECTIONS

surprise and pleasant experiences to customers. This requires a thoughtful and conscious design of your brand so high levels of customer service and genuine attention to customer needs are built into the core of your products and your company as a brand. It's not an easy feat, especially for large companies with complex and fragmented touchpoints, but it is one of the most enduring competitive advantages your company can ever develop.